Lunch with Loretta

DISCOVER THE POWER
OF A MENTORING FRIENDSHIP

Karen Foster

KAREN FOSTER

Discover the Power of a Mentoring Friendship

ISBN 978-0-578-69499-3

Book cover photo and design: Jennifer Wrede

This book is a memoir. While I've done my best to truthfully share our conversations, for dramatic and narrative purposes, I've altered some details and compressed many dialogues and events.

My Goal is God Himself

Francis Brook

My goal is God Himself; not joy, nor peace,
Nor even blessing, but Himself, my God;
'Tis His to lead me there, not mine, but His—
"At any cost, dear Lord, by any road!"

So faith bounds forward to its goal in God,
And love can trust her Lord to lead her there;
Upheld by Him, my soul is following hard,
Till God hath full fulfilled my deepest prayer.

No matter if the way be sometimes dark,
No matter though the cost be ofttimes great,
He knoweth how I best shall reach the mark;
The way that leads to Him must needs be strait.

One thing I know—I cannot say Him nay;
One thing I do—I press toward my Lord,
My God, my glory here from day to day,
And in the glory there my Great Reward.

Dedication

To Loretta Chalfant, I'm so blessed to
call you my mentor and friend.
Thank you for recognizing my hunger for
God and coming alongside me.
Your words and example helped me navigate life.
To the women who told me, "I wish I had a Loretta,"
May God's Spirit use this book to mentor your
heart and draw you closer to himself.

Contents

Personal Invitation

Dear Reader,

Can you think of someone whose life and wisdom shaped your character and helped determine the direction of your life?

Loretta Chalfant is that person for me. Loretta is eighteen years older than I and a hundred years wiser. One day she extended a bold invitation: "I see your desire to go deeper with God. May I come alongside and help you?"

The book you hold in your hands is *not* a "how to" book on spiritual mentoring. Rather, it's a warm re-telling of our lunch conversations as we explored deeper intimacy with God. Loretta's mentoring style wasn't *formal*—we didn't go through a program or study the Bible together, although we often talked about different Scriptures because we both love God's Word.

Mainly we talked of life. Our Dreams. Successes. Disappointments. We sorted through the past and present like women preparing for a garage sale, putting into separate piles what we wanted to keep, throw out, or recycle. I left every lunch with a satisfied heart: a fresh insight, a shift in perspective, a bit of inspiration, or a solid challenge to help me grow as a wife, mom, and a follower of Jesus.

Do you long for that kind of woman-to-woman synergy?

Join us! Pull up a chair. Listen in on the life-changing conversations that happen when friends are vulnerable, honest, and care deeply about one another.

As a bonus, I've included recipes at the end of the book because it seems we always connect best around food. Are you a mentor? A mentee? Either way, these recipes come highly recommended from some pretty fabulous women!

My prayer is that as you gather with friends you'll "taste and see that the Lord is good" and, like me, you'll savor the rich wisdom that comes when we lay bare our hearts to one another and to God.

Bon Appetit!

CHAPTER 1

An Invitation To Go Deeper

This invitation to a meal is an invitation to intimacy with God.
—Henri J. M. Nouwen

My invitation to go deeper with God arrived during sweater weather, a crisp October afternoon, when I least expected it. I can be flighty. Sometimes I forget what I'm reheating in the microwave before the timer beeps at me two minutes later. But I remember that idyllic day as if God had custom-made it just for me.

Red breasted robins had greeted the dawn with their rapid song, "Cheerily, cheer up, cheer up," and by noon were trolling in my northern California lawn for earthworms. The leaves on my dwarf Japanese maples waved in the breeze like thousands of red flags lining a parade route. I wanted to park myself outside and drink up that day like it was a cup of hot Earl Grey tea. But I had too much to accomplish.

I stood in the laundry room mindlessly folding clean socks and underwear when the house phone rang. A familiar, soft-spoken voice greeted me on the answering machine. (This was back in the day when we had home lines and answering machines.)

"Karen, are you there? This is Loretta. I was wondering—"

Loretta . . . from women's Bible Study?

I raced to the kitchen with an armload of laundry and picked up the phone, leaving a trail of mismatched socks on the wooden floor. Loretta invited me to lunch. Then she paused as though summoning courage and said, "I normally wait for someone to ask me about mentoring them, but . . . I felt like God asked me to walk beside you. Are you willing to meet with me on occasion?"

Of course I was willing to meet with Loretta. The thought of meeting with her gave me an adrenaline rush. The same way I'd react if someone knocked on my door and announced, "You've won the Reader's Digest Sweepstake. Here's a check for $50,000!" Loretta inspired me to seek God. But what were those other words attached to her invitation? Did God really ask her "to walk beside me?" She mentioned *mentoring.* Did I really need a spiritual mentor?

I'd been a Christian for forty-two years. I was on fire for God— you should have seen my scorch marks. I led women's Bible studies, worked in a prison ministry, spoke at women's groups, taught children's Sunday school, and volunteered at my kids' private Christian school. But Loretta was eighteen years older than me. Maybe she didn't see me as a spiritually mature Christian. Maybe she thought I needed some strong guidance. Why else would she offer to mentor me? Did she see some flaw in me that she felt needed to be addressed?

I could hear Loretta breathing on the other end of the phone line. How long had she been waiting for an answer?

Why not? If nothing else, I hoped Loretta would share how she coped when her husband died in a plane crash. Like my husband, he had been a pilot. I feared for Dan's safety. Tried not to go there in my head. But from everything I'd observed at church, Loretta was not a bitter or melancholy woman. She exuded the joy of the Lord.

"I'd love to meet with you," I said.

And I really meant it. So why did I inhale after we hung up as though I was about to jump off a high dive into the deep end of the pool?

Two days later I drove along the rural highway that dipped and rose among the towering pine trees as I headed for a small-town bistro. My emotions were like a can of mixed nuts. On one hand I was ecstatic to have one-on-one time with Loretta. I'd known a lot of godly women, but no one who could whet my appetite for a deeper relationship with the Lord the way she did. Whenever she spoke about God during Bible study, flecks of golden light danced in her teary brown eyes. Her words were brief but rang of someone who'd sat at God's feet and *knew* him in a personal way that filled me with awe. Equally endearing, when Loretta spoke to me at church, she looked into my eyes and listened. Really listened. I couldn't wait to spend time with her.

On the other hand, I felt nervous. I'd never been mentored. What did that look like? Would we study the Bible together? Would we discuss how to apply Scripture to our lives? Would Loretta ask me questions and respond with godly advice? My mind went wild. How much of my naked soul did I want to expose? What if I shared something that made Loretta think less of me? What if she judged me for having a glass of wine or for allowing my seven-year-old son to play video games that involved war?

I shook my head in an attempt to free myself of my insecure thoughts. *Chill, Karen. This is a lunch date . . . not a religious inquisition. We're just two women who love God and enjoy talking about Jesus.*

Jesus. I'd first become aware of Jesus when I was a skinny six year old with curly blond hair. Jesus was a one-dimensional, six-inch felt figure (about the size of my paper dolls) attached to a blue flannel graph. I still remember smoothing my pink taffeta dress over my knobby knees while I sat cross-legged on the classroom floor listening to my Sunday school teacher, Mrs. Johnson. She talked about Jesus and how he made a lame man walk. That story made my insides grow warm and deliciously full as though I'd just drunk a mug of hot cocoa.

Mrs. Johnson said something about how we could go to heaven if we asked Jesus to be our Savior. I couldn't spell the word Savior much less understand why I needed one. I was an *innocent* kid who strived to please my folks and who obeyed adult rules as if my life depended on it. So when she asked the class to bow our heads and invite Jesus into our hearts, I did what she asked. I didn't know how Jesus could live in my heart, but I wasn't going to pass up an invitation to go to heaven—wherever that was. When she told us to raise our hand "if you invited Jesus into your heart," I raised my hand.

That was the first time I asked Jesus into my heart. The second time (I guess I wasn't sure my first prayer "took") was in eighth grade. My Sunday school class of gangly adolescents sat on blankets beneath mesquite trees in the Arizona desert and listened to our Sunday school teacher, Major Gray. He talked about his narrow escape from death when the Air Force jet he'd been flying was hit by enemy gunfire during the Vietnam War. "I managed to fly the jet back to our military base but staring death in the face shook me to the core." His deep voice trembled with great emotion. "That day, I asked Jesus to be my Savior. My decision to follow Christ changed the trajectory of my life."

As I listened, all the warm cocoa emotions I'd felt for Jesus during my childhood rushed back, but this time with a new grid. By then I'd had enough schoolgirl drama to know my thirteen-year-old heart wasn't so innocent (nothing like having a friend steal my heartthrob to bring out the cat claws). I needed someone to save me from myself; someone who could promise me eternal life. When the Major asked if we wanted Jesus as our Savior, I thrust my hand skyward like a backward bolt of lightning.

From then on, I stoked the fire in my soul the only way I knew how—with religious activity. My life became a list of ought and should. I ought to read my Bible. I should pray. I ought to tithe. I should treat others as I want to be treated. I ought to share the gospel with nonbelievers. I should serve in church wherever there's a need. I didn't mind the list (although it provoked a huge amount of guilt when I failed to do them) because I loved the Lord and assumed he'd love me more if I did these things. And yet something was missing.

Some days I'd meet with God and his overpowering love and presence would crash down on me like a giant wave, drenching my spirit with indescribable joy. Most days, my quiet time with the Lord was just that—quiet, and unremarkable. I'd pray and wait for God's Spirit to rush in and sweep me off my feet. Instead, his presence ebbed and flowed without fanfare, like a tepid tide that drifted in, tickled my ankles, and slipped back into the sea. I wasn't naïve. I knew it wasn't possible to live on a constant spiritual high. But why couldn't I experience more of God's joy and peace in the ordinary moments? I wanted to be tight with God twenty-four seven. I longed to be in a relationship with him that didn't fluctuate with my circumstances and moods. Steady joy. I wanted that. Loretta seemed to have it. Maybe she'd share her secret.

Loretta had warned me on the phone, "I don't have all the answers. I'm walking out this earthly journey like everyone else." Even so, her countenance told me she *knew* God better than I did. I hoped Loretta would show me how to satiate my ravenous soul (without giving me too much heartburn). At least it was worth a try.

I parked the car on Main Street and hurried to the historical building which now housed a bistro. A large plastic pumpkin with triangular eyes and a toothless grin stared at me from inside the bay window surrounded by a garland of orange and red leaves. I looked at my reflection in the glass. A slender, blue-eyed woman in her late forties stared back at me. I realized that I looked far more mature than I felt on the inside. When would the skinny, insecure girl inside of me catch up to my age? I raked my fingers through my ash-blond bangs and shoulder-length hair.

Here goes. I inhaled deeply and opened the door like a wide-eyed student on the first day of school, nervous, but eager to learn. As I entered the bistro, the scent of freshly baked bread greeted me. I scanned the narrow room. Loretta sat tall next to the interior brick wall with her back to the door. Her cropped silver-white hair was like a crown of wisdom that beckoned me forward.

I tapped her shoulder. "Sorry I'm late."

"Karen, nice to see you." Loretta's smile stretched the small lines around her mouth. She stood and wrapped her arms around me. At five-foot-eleven she was six inches taller than I am and her warm, firm hug made me sigh like I'd just come home.

When we sat down, a stocky waitress with a silver nose stud and a mermaid tattoo on her left forearm came to our table. She handed me a menu and turned to Loretta, who already had a menu and a glass of water. The two of them bantered back and forth like long lost friends while I scanned the menu.

We placed our order, and then Loretta touched the waitress's tattooed arm and said, "Tamara, I hope your ultrasound goes well. I'll be praying."

"That would be awesome. Thanks."

"How do you know that girl?" I asked, after the waitress left.

"I don't," she said. "We only met today."

Unconvinced, I arched an eyebrow.

"It's true." Her eyes brightened. "I enjoy people. I love our differences and similarities. I just have to remind myself to slow down and be available. God never ceases to amaze me with the people he brings along my path."

Mutual, I thought, grateful for Loretta. I didn't realize the impact this woman would make on my life.

"So Loretta, when we spoke on the phone, you talked about mentoring me. I have no idea what that looks like. What exactly do you have in mind?"

"I don't have an agenda," she said, and took a drink of water. "I just want to come alongside you and do life. Get together and talk . . . nothing formal. I see you as hungry for God."

Whew! At least she didn't view me as a make-over project.

"Karen, sometimes I listen to you in Bible study and feel as though I'm looking in the mirror at a younger me. I couldn't get enough of God." Loretta's eyes watered like two brown pools behind her red-framed glasses. "I wanted to be a missionary to the Jewish people."

"And were you?"

"No, my life took a different turn. I met Brian in Greek class at seminary and we fell in love." Loretta didn't wear a wedding ring, but she mindlessly twisted a silver band on her right index finger. Then, she looked at me and sighed. "Shoot bother, where was I?"

I grinned. Whenever Loretta felt flustered, she used that term. "You were explaining why you want to meet with me."

Loretta nodded and her eyes searched mine. "Meeting with you would bless me too. Since I moved here from southern California, I've missed having a friend who enjoys talking about God."

I returned her smile. I knew exactly what she meant. I loved talking about God with my friends. Small talk drove me nuts. Still, the question swirled in my head. *Where do we go from here?* Before I could ask, the waitress arrived with our meal.

Loretta pressed her long fingers against her stomach. "Can you hear my stomach growling? I haven't eaten anything since I went to Taco Bell yesterday afternoon." She leaned forward and whispered, "I'm hooked. I went three times last week."

"Wow! Three times?" I frowned, thinking of all those fast-food calories. "That's a lot of . . . tacos!"

Loretta laughed and reached across the table to clasp my hands. "Shall we pray?"

I bowed my head, noting the wrinkles and age spots on Loretta's hands that differed from my own, youthful hands. Loretta thanked God for the food, praised him for loving and pursuing us, and satisfying our souls with himself. The tone of her voice mesmerized me . . . a blend of adoration and respect. Then, she squeezed my hand and paused. I heard her swallow. When she spoke again, her voice quivered with emotion. "Father, give us teachable hearts and a deeper desire to know you better." My flesh tingled. God's presence was so palatable that I wouldn't have been surprised to hear the scraping against the floor as though he'd just pulled up a chair to join us.

When she said, "Amen," I watched Loretta dab her wet cheeks with a cloth napkin. I didn't feel uncomfortable. Loretta's tears had always come easily whenever she talked about God. That's what I wanted—a heart so in love with Jesus that I cry at the sound of his name.

For the next twenty minutes, Loretta and I chatted about our families. Loretta nibbled on her grilled tuna sandwich as I talked about how I'd grown up as an Air Force brat, graduated from college with a speech major, and joined the Air Force where I'd met Dan, my husband of twenty-four years. I'd left the military to stay home with our kids—boy, girl, boy who were now 18, 16, and 7.

While I savored my spinach, mushroom, and feta cheese quiche, Loretta told me that her eleven-year marriage to Brian had ended in 1972 when he died. Loretta had three children (two sons and a daughter in their thirties and married). She had six grandchildren with another on the way.

I started to ask about Brian's death but before I could bring up the subject, Loretta pushed her empty plate aside and looked me squarely in the eye. "If you don't mind, I'd like to tell you about a prayer that's been dear to my heart for decades."

I sat tall, ready for my first lesson.

"I think our tendency," she said, "is to pray for a safe, pleasant life without bumps."

True. But where was she going with this?

"I want to challenge you to ask God to teach you his lessons—no matter the cost."

Teach me . . . *no matter the cost?*

Hairs stirred on the back of my neck. I could think of many people who had learned God's lessons at an exorbitant price. Our friends, the Blake family, had given up a successful business to become missionaries overseas. Their home had been broken into and the wife died after a painful battle with ovarian cancer.

"Uh, I don't know if I want to say that prayer."

Silence. Was she waiting for an explanation? Disappointed in my answer?

I cleared my throat. "I'm afraid God *will test* me."

Loretta tilted her head and waited for me to continue.

"I know adversity can strengthen our faith," I stuttered. "My biggest spiritual growth spurt happened during a difficult time in my life. But I don't know if I'm up for anything like that right now. What if my husband died—" The remaining words lodged in my throat. I'd forgotten I was talking to a widow.

Loretta touched my hand. "Karen, we don't need to be afraid of God. He's a good and loving Father. Besides, I'd hate to see you worry and dwell on *what ifs* that may never happen."

The warmth of her hand didn't alleviate my fear. I knew God wouldn't cause Dan to die just because I prayed that prayer. Ridiculous! But, could I help it if those imaginary *what ifs* made me overly fearful when it concerned my family? What if my seven-year-old son gets abducted? What if my cheerleader daughter breaks her neck doing acrobatics? What if my college son is in a car wreck? What if my husband gets cancer?

I shrugged. "I probably sound silly . . . or even superstitious, but I feel like I'm inviting trouble if I say that prayer."

"I'm sorry. Maybe I shouldn't ask you to say that prayer." She clasped her hands together on the table. "I see you wanting to go deeper with God and I assumed you were ready for him to teach and change you. Sounds like you're struggling to capture your thoughts."

I looked down and smoothed the cloth napkin on my lap, thankful that no one was sitting close enough to hear our conversation. Maybe I didn't want to be mentored or have her "come alongside me." On the other hand, I welcomed Loretta's no-nonsense approach. I wasn't put off by her challenge to go deeper with God any more than I'd be offended by a physical trainer who pushed me to run one more lap.

"You're right, Loretta. Capturing my thoughts is an ongoing battle. I try to be optimistic, but the world's so dangerous that my mind slips into wild imaginings. That's why that prayer scares me." I cleared my throat. "Do you still say that prayer?"

"Yes, because I know God's eternal purposes are for my good. Even now, whenever I run into something I can't comprehend or that's difficult, my first response is, 'Father, use this to teach me and change me.'" Loretta's face became pensive and she leaned forward. "Karen, trusting God is huge if we're going to ask him to teach us."

Using my index finger, I shoved a black olive around on my otherwise empty plate. The death of a husband, and the responsibility of raising three young kids by herself, seemed like an expensive price tag to me. What on earth did God teach Loretta? Could she honestly say that lesson was worth the cost?

More to the point, were there lessons I didn't want to learn? Areas I refused to submit? I picked up the olive and plopped it into my mouth. *Ohh, why can't I just swallow a spiritual growth pill to make me godly?*

"Loretta, I know God uses our circumstances to teach us. He doesn't need our permission. So what's the point in asking God to teach us?"

"You're right. At the end of the day, we really don't have any control about the lessons we're taught. But, I believe saying that prayer shows God we're willing to surrender control and step out of our comfort zone to learn his lessons." Loretta straightened the silver bracelets on her left wrist. "I also believe that prayer affects how we view our circumstances. Because then, even our worst-case scenarios are seen as an opportunity for God's Spirit to teach us and make us more like Christ."

I swallowed hard, wishing I had a pen and paper to write down Loretta's words. I also thought of several questions. *What did God teach you when your husband died? What is the greatest lesson God taught you?* But Loretta looked at her watch and gasped. "I need to scoot. I have a dentist appointment."

I masked my disappointment and waved at Tamera who brought our check to the table. She started to walk away and then spun back around. "Thanks for offering to pray for me," she told Loretta. "It means a lot."

How does Loretta do it? How is she able to go deep with people so quickly? I got the impression Loretta made everyone she met feel special. That's how I felt. I grabbed the check. "This is my treat."

"What? I invited you to lunch."

"True, but you offered to mentor me. I'd say that's worth the price of a meal—unless of course, you've changed your mind. I'm not the smartest peach in the bunch." I frowned. "Or is it the prettiest peach?"

Loretta's robust laugh made me grin.

I had much to learn from this wise woman. I was already looking forward to our next lunch together. I just hoped I could ask God to teach me his lessons without crossing my fingers.

Take Away Nuggets

 Ask God to teach and change you no matter the cost.

 "I will instruct you and teach you in the way you should go; I will counsel you with my eye upon you" (Psalm 32:8 ESV).

*Food for
Thought*

1. Have you ever had a spiritual mentor, or been a mentor to someone else? If so, what did that relationship look like? If not, what are some possible benefits that would come from such a relationship?

2. Why did Loretta challenge Karen to pray for God "to teach his lessons no matter the cost" rather than ask for a safe life without bumps? What was Karen's reaction? Can you relate to her superstitious fears? How would you respond to Loretta's challenge?

3. Loretta said, "Trusting God is huge if we're going to ask him to teach and change us." Why is it necessary to trust God if we want a deeper relationship with him?

CHAPTER 2

Turn up the Heat

Few people arise in the morning as hungry for God
as they are for cornflakes or toast and egg.
—Dallas Willard

I lit a cinnamon-scented candle in the hall bathroom,
rearranged the throw pillows on my brown leather sofa
(for the second time), and placed an acorn-shaped candy
dish filled with mints on the coffee table. A festive centerpiece of
my own creation, a pot of yellow chrysanthemums nestled in a
hollowed-out pumpkin, adorned my dining room table.

Everything in order and ready for Loretta, I told myself. I was
feeling pretty proud about my hostess skills until the oven timer
beeped. I grabbed a potholder and opened the oven. *No, no, no!*
My homemade pumpkin bread had sunk in the middle, resembling
a bathtub.

"Why today of all days?" I glanced at the oven clock. Loretta
would arrive any minute. I pulled out the pan, scraped my inedible

fiasco into the garbage, and hid the evidence (dirty pan) in the dishwasher.

Why did I invite Loretta over for lunch? I'm no Rachael Ray.

Although I loved having people in my home, cooking for them always flustered me. The unrealistic need to be perfect, I suppose, and the desire to make a good impression. I told myself the dust bunnies didn't matter. Or what I served for lunch. Loretta was coming to see *me*. She cared about my heart—not my house.

Sadly, my heart had been frantic all morning as I'd prepared for her arrival. My handwritten to-do list lay on the snack bar next to my unopened Bible. Need I mention which one had taken priority?

I rummaged in the food pantry for something sweet to replace my doomed pumpkin bread. An open package of orange-filled Oreo cookies caught my eye. My other option? A glass pumpkin jar filled with week-old Halloween candy. *So much for good impressions. Cookies it is.*

Next on my list, prepare the sandwiches. I rushed to the refrigerator and pulled out a serving bowl filled with broccoli salad along with deli meat and condiments just as Loretta hollered through my front screen door.

"Knock, knock."

Eleven a.m. Right on time.

"Come in," I hollered back.

Loretta came around the corner. She squeezed me and said, "Smells like pumpkin in here."

I ignored her comment and waved towards a kitchen stool. "Take a seat. I'm making croissant sandwiches. Are you okay with alfalfa sprouts with your turkey and provolone cheese?"

"Sounds great!"

I washed my hands and wiped them on my apron. I'm fond of aprons. This one had black polka dots on a white background and a lime-green waistband that made me look like I'd stepped out of a 1950s catalogue. Minus the pearl necklace and high heels.

"I'd planned to make chicken tortilla soup," I said, slicing two croissants in half lengthwise, "but November's warm this week." From the kitchen, Loretta could see my dining and living room area. She nodded towards two queen-sized quilts mounted like paintings on the wall opposite my large picture window. The quilt nearest my dining room displayed a burgundy apple motif on an ivory background. The other patchwork quilt had a rustic mountain theme.

"Did you make those?"

"No, I just like decorating with quilts. Adds color to my walls. Makes the room feel cozy." My pride winced as I followed Loretta's eyes. Had she seen the long cobweb clinging from the ceiling to the top of one of the quilts?

"I love country things too," Loretta replied. "I also love the photos on your refrigerator. Is that your family?"

"Yes, it is." I pointed to each face with my butter knife. "This is my husband, Dan, and our three J's—Jonathan, Jenny, and Jason." I waved my knife at a jar of pickles. "Would you like a dill pickle on the side?"

"Yes, please. You know, my youngest son and his family live about forty-five minutes from here. Being around them reminds me how much energy it takes to raise children."

"Definitely keeps me busy." I set the food on the table, poured two glasses of sparkling water, and removed my apron. Then I gestured for Loretta to sit across from me. "Would you mind saying grace?"

Giving thanks for our food was a mere footnote in her gracious God-centered prayer. As I listened to Loretta praise God's goodness, my shoulders relaxed for the first time that day. Whatever I'd written on my to-do list didn't seem important compared to my huge God. Why hadn't I spent time with him first thing this morning instead of scurrying around like a mouse on steroids?

At the end of the prayer, Loretta grinned at her stuffed croissant. "This looks larapin!"

"Uh, never heard that word. What does it mean?"

"Larapin means out-of-this-world good. It's a southern slang word I learned when Brian and I lived in Tennessee. We were only there for two years, but I inherited some quirky sayings that still appeal to my sillier nature. Ask my grands. They've made a list: 'You scramble my eggs.' 'Cornflakes!' 'You're as handy as a pocket on a shirt.'"

I smiled, trying to envision Loretta's silly side. I didn't know she had one. Then again, had she ever witnessed my flaky, blond moments? We were just getting to know each other. I ran my tongue over my teeth, wondering how long you need to know someone before you can be candid and mention there's food stuck between her teeth.

Loretta spooned a generous helping of broccoli salad next to her sandwich. "My son Jeff once said, 'Mom, you're complex. You love to laugh and play games, but you're very intense when it comes to God.' And he's right."

"You may be intense, but it's not like you jump on a soapbox and brow beat people with God's Word. I think your intensity is a reflection of your heartfelt love for God and his joy in you. It's how you express your passion for God."

Loretta smiled and took another bite of her sandwich.

"You asked me to pray about what I want to learn. Remember? I want to know how to experience constant fellowship with God—the kind of oneness that Jesus talks about in John 15."

I expected Loretta to say something like, "Good for you. That's a great lesson to learn." Instead, she quietly ran her fingers around the edge of her water glass. If she wanted my undivided attention, she had it.

"Karen, your desire for constant fellowship with God is good. But, it takes more than desire."

I arched my brow in question.

"Intimacy doesn't happen overnight. Like any relationship, it takes time." Loretta paused to take a drink of water. "It also takes discipline."

I straightened my shoulders. I was disciplined. I'd completed the *Through the Bible in a Year* multiple times. I finished my weekly Bible study homework assignments. I memorized Scripture. Just how much more disciplined did one have to be?

Loretta leaned forward, a challenge issuing from her luminous brown eyes. "How important is it for you to go deeper with God? Because that's what you're asking for. Are you willing to make God a priority over your personal agenda so you can spend time with him every day?"

I'd just bit into a dill pickle, but it was her question that made my face pucker. Didn't I just say I wanted constant fellowship with God? Did she question my intent? I chomped my pickle.

Loretta sighed. "It'd be nice if all it took to have intimacy with God was to read a morning devotion on our way out the door. But it's not that simple if we truly want to know God. We need to be still, *completely still*, before him on a regular basis."

I looked out the sliding glass door in my dining room which adjoined an enclosed glass patio. I enjoyed sitting there on a lounge chair, reading my Bible and listening to the small landscaped waterfall in our backyard. We lived on five acres in the Sierra Foothills. Oaks, manzanita, and pine trees encircled our beige two-story house, and sheltered a diversity of loquacious birds. Fresh evergreen pine scent filled the air. Sometimes God's presence seemed so tangible, I'd weep for the joy of it.

But more often than not, I'd settle into the lounge chair and my mind would wander. Instead of tuning my spirit into his presence, I'd notice the cat hair on the footstool, the red dirt on the patio floor, the sticky fingerprints on the sliding glass door. The taskmaster in me would win out. I'd jump out of the lounge chair and pray while I swept, worship while I watered the plants, and talk to God while I cleaned the litter box. I told myself God didn't mind as long as I talked with him as I did my tasks.

Loretta interrupted my reverie. "The Spirit of God needs space to speak into our lives. Don't you find it difficult to multitask and truly listen?"

Yikes, was the woman a mind-reader?

"Psalm 46:10 says, 'Cease striving and know that I am God.' That verse inspires me," Loretta said, then took a bite of her broccoli salad. "Some other translations say, 'Be still, and know that I am God.'"

This was feeling a bit convicting. Maybe if I shifted the focus back to her . . . "What does being still look like for you, Loretta?"

"First I have to admit to myself that I can't practice God's presence on the run. I can't worship him and experience intimacy by rushing in and pouring out a bunch of words."

Good point, but hard to practice.

"I've also learned that being still isn't just about making myself sit still long enough to relax. I have to quiet my mind by singing worship songs, or whatever it takes, so I can get my eyes off myself. Off my needs, my feelings, my worries."

"Go on."

"Every morning, I'm faced with the same choice. Do I spend time with God or hurry and get on with my personal business? Left unchecked, my natural tendency is to please myself. When I listen to *me*, I get less of *him*."

Loretta cleared her throat and took a drink, which gave me a moment to savor her words.

"When I choose to be still and meet with God," she continued, "there's a profound peace that comes with his companionship. I'm able to go through my day without worrying about the human stuff of life because it's not on the surface. I'm in a place of peace, confident God's right there. You know?"

I nodded and thought about the last time I'd experienced "God-right-there." Instead of tackling my to-do list, I'd opened my Bible and read Isaiah 40:28 aloud. "Have you never understood? The Lord is the everlasting God, the Creator of all the earth. He never grows weak or weary. No one can measure the depths of his understanding."

When I got to verse 31, I felt as though God gathered me in his loving arms as I read "But those who trust in the Lord will find new strength. They will soar high on wings like eagles." A warmth had spread like rich molasses throughout my whole body until my spirit soared as though God had set me on an eagle's wings. I wanted to stay that way all day—caught up in that holy moment.

I smiled at Loretta as I recalled that moment, wondering if the heat of it showed on my face now. I touched my cheeks, surprised that my skin felt cool.

"I love being smack dab in the middle of God's sacred space," I said, "but getting to that place isn't easy. Even when I make time to be alone with God, my thoughts zip here and there. Like a dog chasing after a squirrel."

"I hear you," Loretta groaned. "I have to work at it too. I woke up this morning and realized I'd had so much on my mind that I'd been distracted for the past few days. I hadn't given the mental energy needed to engage God beyond a surface level. When I went to my chair to be still, the subtle thought came, 'I don't want to take the time.' Even so, I quieted my mind and fought those distractions so I could connect spirit to Spirit with God."

I thought about my own failure to follow through this morning as I took a slow sip of water.

"If I want more of God," Loretta added, "I have to do the work of drawing near in true submission."

"I should write this down so I don't forget." I went to the kitchen for a pen and paper, and the bottle of sparkling water to refill our glasses. When I sat down, Loretta seemed pensive.

"Karen, may I ask you a personal question?"

What now? You've already gotten pretty personal. But something in my spirit told me to trust her. I nodded. She searched my eyes, long and hard. I got the impression she was peeling back the layers of my heart like an onion. A thin film of tears formed over her eyes.

"I've only known you for a year. Correct me if I'm wrong. From what you've shared, it seems you're more preoccupied with *doing things* for God than *being still*. Would you agree?"

I thrust my chin at her. "What's wrong with doing things for God? Even Jesus kept busy doing things for God. He healed people, taught in the temple, fed people."

Loretta said nothing so I continued, certain my powerful logic was the reason for her silence.

"I read, just the other day, how Jesus healed a lame man on the Sabbath. When the Jewish leaders got after him for breaking the law, Jesus defended his actions by saying his Father was at work so he was working too." I folded my arms across my chest. "So it seems doing things for God is worthy."

"Our worth is in God, not in our good deeds." Loretta repositioned her glasses. "Besides, how can we know what we're supposed to be doing for God, or be an effective doer, unless we're alone with him long enough to listen?"

I took my fork and repeatedly poked the defenseless broccoli floret on my plate while Loretta continued speaking. Her voice grew more intense with each sentence.

"As for Jesus, he's the perfect example of someone who had unbroken fellowship with God the Father. Jesus went to a solitary place to pray first thing in the morning before he talked to people or performed miracles. After Jesus fed the crowd, he went to the mountains by himself to pray." Loretta pointed to heaven and then herself. "If Jesus needed to commune with God, to hear his voice and obey God's will, why would I choose to live differently?"

No argument there. I set my fork over the mutilated broccoli.

"Karen, I struggle with being still. I'm not kidding when I say it took me fifteen years to learn how to die to self and live mindful of God's presence. And then, practice, practice, practice his presence."

Fifteen years? *Holy guacamole!* I pictured myself, 110 years old, sitting in a wheelchair with a blanket over my lap as I declared to my nurse, "I got it! I've finally learned to live in unbroken fellowship with God."

I studied Loretta's face, the clear light in her eyes, the way she smiled so easily. I wanted the kind of intimacy she had with God but I wasn't sure it was possible for me in this season of life. "My life is jam-packed. Until I have an empty nest like you, my life isn't slowing down," I said more defensively than I intended.

"We *all* have responsibilities. We all have choices."

Score! In our tennis volley of words, Loretta had effectively slammed the ball on the baseline. Fifteen—Love. Instead of quitting while she was ahead, Loretta kept on serving—one truth after another.

"If we wait for life to slow down before we choose to be still before God, an entire lifetime will slip away. Honestly, I'm selfish enough that I want to enjoy God and experience his best for me today. I don't want to wait for a tomorrow that may never come."

Everything she said was true. So what was this thread of resistance in me? Did I really take so much pride in my "doing" that I didn't want instruction about it? I pushed past the resistance and leaned forward.

"I'm listening."

"Learning to be conscious of God's presence, even in a crowd, is not only heavenly . . . it is fundamental to a deeper relationship with God." Loretta pushed her chair from the table and crossed her long legs. "Plus the way I see it, the benefits of being with God aren't just about experiencing his peace and joy. He helps me do what needs to be done. My perspective changes dramatically. I see as God sees, and hopefully feel what he feels toward others."

The air in the room seemed heavy, charged with emotion. Neither of us spoke. The only sound was the *tick, tick, tick* of my kitchen clock's second hand advancing forward.

Loretta uncrossed her legs and leaned forward. "Someone once told me, 'To the degree that we *want* God, is the degree that we'll seek him.'"

I scribbled down her words on the paper in front of me. Underlined them twice.

"You're right, Loretta. The benefits of being still before God overrule my excuses. Bottom line. I refuse to settle for a plain-vanilla faith. I want more of God."

Loretta opened her mouth to speak, but I held up my finger. "Hold that thought. We need a sweet tooth fix."

I went to my walk-in pantry for the cookies—and a reprieve. As I reached for the package of Oreo cookies, I suddenly remembered my sunken pumpkin bread and the oven. *Did I turn it off?* I hurried to the oven. Sure enough the temperature panel glowed 350 degrees. I hit the off button. So easy to adjust the degree of heat in an oven—just hold down the button for a few seconds. Wish it were that simple for me. Wish I could press a button and increase the degree of my desire for God. I returned to the table with the cookies and a more tender spirit.

"What were you about to say?"

Loretta shook her head. "I've said enough. I trust God's Spirit to teach you what I failed to explain."

I picked up a cookie and carefully separated the two chocolate wafers that sandwiched the orange icing. "I understand. *Being still* is one part of having a relationship with God, and *doing things* for him is the other part." I compared the two round wafers in my hands. One of them looked black and smooth. The other wafer had orange icing on one side. I stuck them together again. "The combination and balance of these two parts achieve the best result—like an Oreo, right?"

"You got it, kiddo!" Loretta grabbed a cookie. "Just remember, this is the stuff God's taught me. He could be doing something entirely different in your life."

"Well, whatever God is teaching me, I know the lessons aren't a slam dunk. Otherwise we wouldn't be having this conversation. Like you said, 'being still before God and mentally engaging him takes practice!'"

When my wall clocked chimed twice, Loretta looked at her watch to verify the time. "Two o'clock already? I need to scoot out of here before your kids get home from school."

"They won't be home for another hour. Please stay!"

She stood and carried her plate and glass to the sink. "I love being with you, but I'd rather you have a few minutes to yourself to think about what we've discussed."

Loretta ignored my groan as I followed her outside, and down the redwood porch steps to her Honda Accord.

"Thank you for lunch," she said, hugging me. "It truly was larapin!"

After Loretta drove away, I hurried inside to clean up the kitchen. I looked at the sink piled with dishes. I looked at the unopened Bible on the counter.

To the degree that we want God, is the degree that we'll seek him.

Time to turn up the heat.

Take Away Nuggets

To the degree that you want God, is the degree that you'll seek him.

"You will seek me and find me, when you seek me with all your heart" (Jeremiah 29:13 ESV).

Food for Thought

1. Do you struggle to be still in God's presence? If so, what keeps you from getting to that sacred place? What can you do to change that?

2. According to author Linda Dillow, "One of the biggest and most common mistakes a woman makes is to substitute activity for God for a relationship with him." Loretta observed in Karen a tendency to do things for God rather than to be still before him. Why do you think Loretta was so adamant about this?

3. On a scale of one to ten (with one being "not at all" and ten being "with intense fervency") how hard do you seek God? What could you do to turn up the heat?

4. Read Matthew 11:28-30. Consider why Jesus said, "Take my yoke upon you. Let me teach you, because I am humble and gentle at heart, and you will find rest for your souls." If you're caught up in a performance-oriented faith, ask Jesus to teach you how to rest in him.

CHAPTER 3

Why, God?

Faith is simply trusting the character of God
even when life gives you reasons not to.
—Corrie Ten Boom

*L*oretta waved a French fry in the direction of the Super Cub airplane sitting on the tarmac. "That's similar to the plane that Brian flew when he was in aviation school," she said.

Today's lunch with Loretta was on the lattice-covered patio at our regional airport. We watched small aircraft take off and land amidst the clatter of forks and the chatter of folks. The smell of grilling hamburgers floated from the cafe's kitchen window. Sparrows flitted beneath the tables in search of crumbs. My heart was deliciously full. I inched my chair closer to Loretta, glad to be with my mentor after not seeing her for a month.

"Did you ever fly with him?" I asked.

"We only flew together three times. It was fun, but the plane rattled so much I felt like I was riding in a tin can full of bolts."

Her laughter drew admiring glances from two white-haired gentlemen at the table next to us. Loretta was an attractive woman. Her statuesque posture and bright, enthusiastic spirit invited others to notice her even though she was too modest to ever think of herself as anything special.

"Did you ever think of marrying again after Brian died?"

Loretta shrugged. "My kids were young, and I didn't want someone else raising them. I'd heard too many horror stories about blended families. I made up my mind to be a single parent. Once the kids were grown, it seemed too late."

I nodded towards the men next to us. "It's never too late."

She glanced over her shoulder and then back at me.

"Weird Margaret," she said, shaking her head.

I smiled when I heard Loretta use her pet phrase for people who say or do something silly. By the blush on her high cheek bones, I knew I'd embarrassed her.

"I haven't ruled marriage out, but neither do I need a man to be happy." Loretta looked at the finger where her wedding ring would have been. "Besides, God surprised me when he brought Brian into my life when I was twenty-four. He can bring someone into my life now that I'm in my sixties . . . if he chooses. That thought keeps me content."

"Speaking of Brian," I emptied a pack of artificial sweetener into my iced tea. *Dare I open the subject?* "You've never told me about his death."

"Brian died when he was 33 on November 12 . . . the same date as our daughter's birthday.

Same date?

I choked on a bacon bit.

Loretta watched me gulp down my tea. Then, her brow furrowed and her mood shifted gears as though she was about to ride a bike uphill to a hard and difficult place. I wondered if discussing Brian's death took more energy than she wanted to exert.

She sat quietly, then a wistful look filled her eyes. Her mind seemed to pedal back in time to that fateful day. I traveled with her and imagined Loretta in her thirties again. Her cropped silver-white hair morphed into a brown bouffant, and the wrinkles that formed the commas at the corner of her eyes vanished. Once again, she was the bustling mother of three young children, the playful wife of a strapping young pilot.

"It was a cool Sunday morning," she said. "I woke at dawn, pulled on a pair of jeans and a sweatshirt, and made breakfast for Brian."

"Where was he going?"

"To work. I think I told you that we were planning to be missionaries overseas with Mission Aviation Fellowship. Brian needed more flight hours, so he designed an aerial patrol plan and offered it to Fort Tejon Ranch in southern California. They owned almost 300,000 acres and needed someone to monitor hunters on their land during the hunting season. In fact, that Sunday was his last scheduled flight with them."

Last flight? The cold irony of that made me shiver.

"I remember that morning like it was yesterday. I stood in our driveway and watched Brian pull on a flannel-lined jacket. A recent storm had dumped snow over the mountain range where he'd be flying and as always, he'd planned ahead for the colder weather." Loretta dipped a French fry in a pool of catsup on her plate.

"Did I ever mention Marty? He went with Brian that day."

I shook my head. "You haven't told me anything."

"Marty was the ranch manager's sixteen-year-old son. He'd flown with my husband the day before as his backseat observer to help him look for poachers. Only it had been too windy to land at the ranch where Marty lived, so they flew to the airport near our house and he spent the night with us."

Did Marty die too? I wanted to ask, but I told myself to be quiet and listen.

"That morning, I watched the two of them squeeze into our old, faded VW bug. The car wasn't much to look at. It had been in a fire and Brian had purchased the pathetic thing for fifty bucks.

"Anyway," Loretta continued, "I must have been in a silly mood. I kept leaning through the driver's window and planting little kisses on Brian's mustache."

I smiled as I imagined cool, no-nonsense Loretta being a playful wife.

"Brian grinned at Marty and said, 'Loretta has a thing about my mustache.' I blushed, but he was right. I did love his mustache." She sighed and pressed her hand against her chest. "And I'm glad for all my foolishness that morning. I waved goodbye as they drove away. That mental snapshot was my final memory of Brian."

Loretta paused. Her eyes drifted towards the yellow Tail Dragger plane. I assumed she was thinking of Brian, but I was thinking of Dan, my husband, who was also a pilot. As a young bride, I'd romanticized the idea of being married to an Air Force pilot, but over the years, I grew to fear for his life. When a plane crashed near our military base, I wept in Dan's arms while he tried to assure me that flying was safer than driving. Now that he flew for the airlines, I breathed easier. And yet, the events of 9/11 made me embrace Dan all the more tightly when he left on a flight. What would I do if his plane crashed? How could I live without him?

"Loretta, we don't have to talk about this now if—"

"I'm okay. I was just remembering how God prepared my heart that day. After Brian left, I loaded the kids in the car and drove to church. During Sunday school, God nudged me to go home and pray for my husband. Not for his safety or for a particular need, but to pray for him in general."

"Really? Did that raise any red flags for you?"

"I was more puzzled than alarmed because I often prayed that way for Brian. Anyway, I did pray. Then, I spent the rest of the afternoon reading a book by Merlin Carothers called *Prison to Praise.*" Loretta slowly shook her head. "I had no idea how instrumental the message of that book would be in the coming days. It challenged me to praise God despite my grief."

Uhh, praising God in grief? I couldn't imagine having an attitude of praise if it had been *my* husband who had died.

"Only to say, I was reading when I looked at my watch and saw it was 5:30. Brian had always said if he wasn't home by that time to call the ranch and locate him. We didn't have cell phones then, you know."

"That's true," I replied. "Did you panic? I would have."

"Not at first. I told myself that he'd stopped on the way home to run an errand, or he'd had car trouble. I fully expected Brian to walk through the door at any moment. And I'd smother his mustache with kisses. When I didn't hear from him by six o'clock, I knew something was wrong."

I set my fork down and leaned forward.

"I called the ranch office, but the secretary claimed she wasn't aware of any problems. That came as a huge relief. What she didn't tell me is that they'd already contacted the sheriff and a rescue helicopter was searching the area, trying to find Brian's plane."

Loretta pushed her now clean plate to the side. "I suppose the secretary didn't want to alarm me. I sat for another hour by the phone, my mind on high alert."

My stomach did a slow roll. It didn't take much imagination for me to be in Loretta's shoes. I could almost hear a second hand ticking as the minutes dragged by. The same way I felt whenever anyone in my family didn't arrive home when they said they would.

"Then the doorbell rang. I ran to it, opened it, and there stood a young man dressed in a starched sheriff's uniform. My heart pounded in my chest. I looked past him, searching the night for my husband. When I didn't see him, my legs turned to jelly and I gripped the door.

"The sheriff said Brian's plane had gone down in the Tehachapi Mountains about sixty miles from our home. They didn't know about Brian's status, but they told me that Marty had survived. He had a broken arm and was in shock, but he'd managed to crawl out of the plane and walk to a hunter's cabin to summon help."

"Wait a second," I interrupted Loretta. "I don't understand. Was Brian alive when Marty left the plane?"

Loretta shrugged. "Like I said, Marty was in shock. He wasn't certain, but he thought maybe Brian was alive and unconscious. The sheriff told me the rescue team was doing their best to find the plane, but because it had snowed the previous day, it made searching for a white plane difficult."

I reached across the table and grabbed Loretta's hand. "Ohhh! You must have been horrified . . . not knowing."

Loretta's voice sank to a gravelly whisper. "I wouldn't let my mind go there. Marty had survived so I had a reason to hope until someone told me otherwise."

I nodded, even though I knew her story didn't have a happy ending.

"I asked the sheriff to come inside and stay with me while I called a friend. Joyce rushed over, and soon, I had a house full of people praying."

"Where were your kids?"

"They'd been innocently playing all afternoon. Honestly, I don't remember what I told them or when. I was in shock. They knew Daddy's plane was lost, but I don't know how much they understood. They were 9, 7, and 6. I remember they wanted to all sleep together that night, so I put down mats and they slept on the floor."

"Did you sleep with them?"

"I laid beside them until they fell asleep. Then, I got up and went to my bedroom so I could be alone and process what was happening. I kept telling myself that if Brian was alive, he'd survive. He'd been trained in survival skills. He would know what to do in the wilderness by himself. But with each passing hour, I became more realistic that I might never see him again."

Loretta swallowed and looked at the cumulus clouds gathering over the distant Sierra Nevada Mountains.

"As I waited for news, a rush of images of Brian paraded through my mind. Him sitting beside me at church and squeezing my leg three times which meant 'I love you.' The sound of his dreamy voice as he read *The Call of the Wild* to our three children while, one by one, they fell asleep across his outstretched body on the living room floor. But, the sweetest memory of all had to do with Winnie the Pooh."

"Winnie the Pooh?"

"Yes. Did I ever tell you that Brian read *Winnie the Pooh* book to me on our honeymoon? Can you imagine?"

"Pooh over love poems?" I teased, relieved to see her smile.

"Actually, he did write me poetry. Brian had the mind of an engineer, a heart for God, and the soul of a poet. And he was playful."

"I also heard he had a sexy mustache," I added.

"That too!" She titled her head back and laughed. "The night before Brian left, Marty came with us to Shakey's Pizza Parlor. Our daughter and youngest son had birthdays within three days of each other, so we had a joint celebration."

My mind reeled. *Two children's birthdays—the same week as Brian's death? How could they celebrate birthdays each year without remembering Brian's accident and mourning his death?*

"Before we left for Shakey's, Brian told Marty, 'I don't believe you've been properly introduced to our family. I'm commonly known as Papa Pooh, this is Mama Pooh, and these are the Pooh children: Pooh Bird, Pooh Bear, and Sister Sue Pooh.'"

Loretta sighed. "It's funny, but precious, to remember how Winnie the Pooh was present at the beginning and end of our married life."

"Like bookends," I said, blinking back tears.

"Like bookends," she echoed. Loretta's tears came, shining like glass. I handed her a clean napkin and felt the weight of her loss as if it were my own. The image of my own three children flashed before me. Which is worse? A widow's grief? Or a mother watching her young children grieve for their father?

I grabbed another napkin to wipe my own eyes and listened as Loretta continued her story.

"Monday afternoon, the phone rang. There were people in the house, but you could hear a pin drop when I answered the phone. And yet, I could barely hear the man's voice over the blood pounding in my ears. He told me that they'd found the plane. Brian was dead."

Loretta laced her fingers together, then laid them in her lap. "After that phone call, my mind went numb for about two hours. Shock I suppose. When I came to, I got up from the chair I was sitting in and said, 'Father God, take us forward from here.'"

I saw our waitress heading toward us with a water pitcher. I shook my head.

"You said you never saw Brian again. Didn't you have to—?"

"Brian's mother identified his body. She needed to see him. I didn't. I wanted to remember Brian as he was that day, laughing as he waved goodbye."

Loretta tossed a bread crumb to a black bird who'd been pacing the brick planter beside us. He grabbed it with his beak and flew away.

Suddenly, I felt angry. It all felt wrong. Poor Loretta was left to raise her three kids by herself. And all Brian wanted to do was to serve God. They were headed for the mission field. *Why God? Why did you allow this godly man to die?*

"Loretta, I hate to ask, but did you . . . do you . . . ever ask God why he allowed your husband to die?"

"I'm not a *why* person," she responded matter-of-factly and tucked a strand of hair behind her ear.

Not ask why? How could you not?

I raised my brows.

"It's true. The way I see it, how can you be a person who trusts God explicitly and then ask him why?"

My pulse shot up. Her question rattled me. I'd never considered that asking "why" could be viewed as flagrant distrust in God.

"I'm not sure it's as simple as that, at least not for me. I would ask 'why.' It's natural to question why bad things happen, especially when they happen to people like you, who were sold out for God."

"God welcomes our questions, but he doesn't have to justify his actions."

I pulled back into my chair. *Is that what I'm doing?*

Loretta looked me square in the eye. "Karen, how can I make you understand? I'd spent the last ten years before Brian's death learning to trust God with some pretty heavy stuff. I'd lived with my husband's brief depression, and my children had critical health issues which I haven't told you about. I had to walk by faith, one step at a time, before I could say with complete confidence that God was the Absolute Controller of all things."

As I drove home, I replayed our conversation.

Would I trust God without question if Dan died? I honestly don't know. I'd probably wallow in self-pity and sink into such an abyss of despair that I couldn't pray, much less accept God's sovereign will.

So how on earth did Loretta trust God with Brian's death? Was it humanly possible? I believed Loretta was telling me the truth, but seriously, how did she tuck her fatherless children into bed each night without inwardly groaning, "Why, God? Why did you take a God-fearing man like Brian who only wanted to serve you? What's the point?"

How did Loretta look at the metal drums she'd been packing for their move overseas and not feel abandoned—or betrayed—by the benevolent God she trusted?

I just didn't get it.

Somehow, Loretta had come to a place of complete surrender, a place of solid, unquestionable trust in God. If Loretta knew how to trust God without having the answers, I needed to know how she got there. I'd ask her pointblank the next time we had lunch.

Take Away Nuggets

 God welcomes your questions, but he doesn't have to justify his actions.

 "He who is the blessed and only Sovereign, the King of kings, and Lord of lords" (1 Timothy 6:15 ESV).

Food for Thought

1. Loretta accepts God's will without question. Karen is a question-asker. When faced with a tragedy, how does spiritual maturity influence our response? How might various personality types respond differently?

2. Think of a time you experienced a deep loss. How did this affect your relationship with God? How did the experience change you?

3. Proverbs 3:5 says, "Trust in the Lord with all your heart; do not depend on your own understanding." How did Loretta demonstrate trust in God when she learned of Brian's death? Give examples of how you are currently seeking to trust God rather than leaning on your own understanding.

CHAPTER 4

Baby Steps

Faith don't come in a bushel basket, Missy. It come one step at a time. Decide to trust him for one little thing today, and before you know it, you find out he's so trustworthy you be putting your whole life in his hands.—Lynn Austin

I snapped apart my fortune cookie and read aloud from the tiny piece of paper tucked inside. "A light heart carries a person through hard times."

Loretta laughed. "If only it were that simple."

I smiled in agreement. We'd just gorged ourselves on egg drop soup and lemon chicken but lunch wasn't over, not by a long shot. I still had to talk to Loretta about something she'd said the last time we were together, the question that had been bugging me for weeks.

"Speaking of hard times." I waved the slip of paper in my hand. "Last time we met we talked about Brian's death and you asked me 'how can you be a person who trusts God explicitly and then ask him why?' Remember?"

"I remember."

"Well, I'm not buying it. If I ask God why bad things happen, it doesn't mean that I trust him any less. Does it?"

The lines between Loretta's brow deepened. "I suppose it depends on your attitude and motives. When you ask, are you demanding that God *justify* why he allows difficult times?"

I blinked three times. She'd mentioned this the last time we'd met.

"I expect we all question God at some point in our lives," she continued. "When we do, it helps to ask, 'What's the motive behind my questioning?' I think it was Elisabeth Elliot who said, 'Faith does not eliminate questions. But faith knows where to take them.'"

"I like that!" I snatched a pen from my purse and jotted the words on the back of an old receipt. Then, I pointed my pen at Loretta. "Only, you *didn't* question God when Brian died. How did you come to that place of complete trust?"

Loretta studied her fingernails for a moment, then looked at me. "I'll tell you. But first, I have a question for you."

"Ask away."

"Did you ever go through a hard time when you had to trust God?"

"Of course." My heartbeat quickened. "I had three miscarriages in two years when I was in my mid to late thirties . . . around twelve years ago."

Loretta's face softened. "Three? Oh, Karen, that had to be so difficult. What did you do? Did you turn to God? Or did you turn away from him?"

"Both."

I looked away and watched the Koi fish swim aimlessly back and forth in a huge aquarium next to the cash register. Sometimes, I felt that way—wishy washy—when I tried to trust God.

"Jonathan and Jenny were four and two when I became pregnant with our third child. Dan and I were thrilled. Our kids couldn't wait to have another sibling. But I miscarried at eight weeks. It may sound morbid, but I saved some of the tissue from our baby and buried it beneath a pine tree in our backyard. I didn't know if it was a boy or a girl so I gave the baby a name that could go either way—Jessie."

Empathy flickered in Loretta's brown eyes.

"Losing that baby made me determined to have another child. I got pregnant within a few months, but my hopes were dashed when I started bleeding at twelve weeks."

In an instant, my mind flashed to that moment when I lay on the examination table looking up into the eyes of the technician performing the ultrasound. Her expressionless face, lit up from the glow of the screen, alarmed me as she searched my womb for signs of life. Tears welled in her eyes. Slowly she shook her head and said, "I'm sorry. There's no heartbeat."

No heartbeat? When I heard those words, I felt like my own heart had stopped. A few moments later I sat in the lobby waiting to speak with the doctor. Two pregnant women sat across from me. I remember looking at their round bellies that promised life and touching my own flat stomach which felt like a grave. *God, it's not fair. Did I do something wrong?*

I cleared my throat when I realized Loretta couldn't read my thoughts. She'd been waiting for me to speak. "I didn't have a baby to bury so I christened that child with the name, Noel/Noelle, because we'd conceived near Christmas. Dan tried to comfort me. He laid in bed and held me. But that night I couldn't sleep. I got out of bed and went to the living room to read my Bible. I hoped the Holy Spirit would ease my grief. He did. Psalm 27:13-14 says, 'Yet I am confident I will see the Lord's goodness while I am here in the land of the living. Wait patiently for the Lord. Be brave and courageous. Yes, wait patiently for the Lord.'

"I felt confident both my unborn children were in heaven. I could wait, knowing one day I'd be with them. I got on my knees and told the Lord, 'I don't know why this happened, but I believe in your goodness. I trust you to give me another child in your time. If not, I trust you to fill this void in my heart with your peace.'"

I fished a crumpled tissue from my jean pocket and blotted my eyes.

"So you turned *to* God during that miscarriage rather than *away* from him."

"Yes, but as time rolled by and I didn't get pregnant, I questioned God's fairness again. 'Why do you close my womb—a married woman who is devoted to you—and allow a single woman on meth to give birth?' Or I'd see a woman pushing a stroller and ask, 'Why did you answer her prayers and not mine?' Then, after my two best friends gave birth to healthy babies, my initial envy turned to bitterness. I distanced myself from God and turned to other things to take the edge off my pain . . . books, music, movies, wine."

Loretta nodded. Even though she wasn't one to ask God why, I saw no indication that she expected me to respond the same way.

"A year later, I became pregnant, but I wouldn't let myself get excited because I couldn't handle another loss. I raised my fists and told God, 'It's a *cruel joke* if this pregnancy ends in another miscarriage.' I didn't tell anyone, other than Dan, that I was pregnant. And I didn't want to bond with this baby for fear that something would happen."

Before I could finish speaking, the waiter came and removed our plates and left the check without saying a word. But that short commercial break made me assess how much I wanted to share with Loretta. She didn't need to hear the gruesome details of that sorrowful week. The blade to my heart when I first saw the bright red blood on my panties. How I pulled thick skin over my heart so I could go about my business while my body cramped and expelled any hope of new life. I thought I'd cope better if I pretended I was just having a heavy menstrual cycle, but my heart knew it was a lie.

"What happened?" Loretta put her palm against her cheek like someone bracing for bad news.

"I lost the baby at eight weeks," I said point-blank like it didn't matter, but it did.

"Oh, Karen!" Loretta reached over and squeezed my hand. For a moment she was silent, as if she were trying to absorb the pain in me so I didn't have to carry it alone. Finally she spoke. "Did you give that baby a name?"

A name?

My shoulders slumped, feeling the fractured place in my heart.

"No," I breathed. And my words came out in a brittle sound that I didn't recognize. "I *never did* memorialize that baby. I was too mad at God and self-absorbed. I'd stopped reading my Bible. I'd stopped praying. I went to church, but I volunteered in children's ministry so I wouldn't have to listen to sermons talking about 'the goodness of God.' I stayed away from God, even though I knew deep down he was the only one who could help me.

"One night, about six weeks after that third miscarriage, I curled up in a fetal position in my recliner and cried myself to sleep. Hours later I woke up to a pitch-dark living room, except for a tiny red light on our smoke detector. My chest felt tight. The room's walls seemed to close in on me. I stared at that speck of light and silently screamed, 'Help me Lord! I don't deserve your mercy after I've accused you of not loving me and taking my child's life. But, I need you right now like I've never needed you before.'"

A blast of cold air blew through the restaurant as a couple opened the front door. Loretta and I shivered. I slid my flannel jacket over my shoulders.

"Go on," Loretta said. "Did anything happen after you prayed that prayer?"

I nodded. "That night, I stopped bargaining with God to get what I wanted. And I conceded that if I got everything I wanted and didn't have him, I wouldn't be satisfied."

"I love your heart for God." Loretta smiled. "But, if I'm not mistaken, God *did* answer your heart's cry."

I grinned. "Yes, he did. *After* I learned to be content with my family of four . . . and *after* I gave away all my maternity clothes and baby furniture . . . I had Jason, the baby I'd prayed for."

Loretta leaned back in her chair. "Isn't that just like God—to satisfy our deepest longings *after* we've finally surrendered everything to him?"

I nodded and picked up the oriental teapot to refill my cup. It felt awkward to talk about myself so much, but now I saw that mentoring included Loretta drawing things out of me that I didn't know were there, or that I'd forgotten. I hadn't told her about what happened after I gave birth to Jason. This was as good a time as any.

"After those three miscarriages, you can imagine how happy we all were the day that Jason was born. But there was a problem. He couldn't breathe on his own. He needed a ventilator machine to breath for him until an enzyme called surfactant kicked in and lubricated his lungs." I rubbed my chest. "I remember watching Jason's tiny body as he lay in the hospital bassinet with spaghetti wires attached to his jaundiced chest. A ventilator tube ran down his tiny throat. He'd whimper instead of cry. I'd sit in a chair beside him, my swollen breasts filled with milk, desperate to hold him but I couldn't because of all that equipment keeping him alive."

"How long was he in the hospital?"

"Two weeks. I'll never forget the day I got to hold him for the first time. I put on a hospital gown, opened in the front, and leaned back in a recliner. It took two nurses, twenty minutes, to maneuver all the wires and breathing tube so they could lay Jason face down on my chest. Skin to skin."

I swallowed the tears in the back of my throat as I remembered his soft peach-fuzz skin pressed against my chest.

"When I felt Jason's beating heart next to mine, a wave of peace flowed over me as though someone had poured warm lavender oil on my skin. I wrapped my arms around Jason's frail body and embraced him. Then, I did something I never imagined I could do." I cleared my throat. "I released Jason to God. I prayed, 'Thank you for letting me hold my baby. I can let go now, if that's your will.'"

Loretta shivered. "Gives me goosebumps."

"I can't explain it, but when I surrendered my son, it felt like a stream of courage flowed into me from God. My fear turned into faith and carried me through the next ten days. Praise God, Jason arrived home in time to ring in the New Year."

"That's a very happy ending to a very dramatic few weeks," Loretta said. "God was gracious to teach you to trust him through the bearing and loss of your children. He did the same for me."

"Oh yes. I think you mentioned something about your children the last time we met? Tell me."

Loretta took off her glasses and rubbed the depressions on each side of her nose. It was so quiet I could hear dishes clinking in the kitchen. Loretta replaced her glasses and a shadow settled on her face. I knew we were about to travel once again into her past.

"When I married Brian, I didn't know I had a condition called 'infantile uterus' which made getting pregnant near impossible. The doctor prescribed some medication that was supposed to help with fertility. Instead, it made me hemorrhage. I stopped taking the medicine, but the doctor warned me that if I didn't conceive right away, we'd probably never have a child. So we were tickled pink when I became pregnant and had a baby boy."

I smiled, knowing this was a private miracle for her.

Loretta's eyes brightened as if he'd been born yesterday. "I was over the moon happy the day Jay was born. I sat in that hospital bed and examined every inch of his beautiful body. Then, my stomach did a flip-flop. I noticed something wrong with his head. You know those soft spots where you can almost feel the pulse on the top of a baby's head?"

I nodded.

Loretta ran her fingers over her scalp. "Well, I couldn't find them on his head. The pediatrician told me there wasn't a problem, but a month later, Jay was diagnosed with a rare birth defect called Craniosynostosis."

"What's that?"

"Basically, there were no soft spots, which meant there wasn't enough space for his brain to develop. In the 1960s, physicians knew very little about the condition, other than brain damage was inevitable unless we did something to correct the problem."

My eyes widened. "What did you do?"

"Brian and I were paralyzed. However, God was in the lead. Through a miraculous set of circumstances, we were able to get an appointment with the assistant head neurosurgeon at Children's Hospital. By then, Jay was looking quite Mongoloid because his brain was pushing against every conceivable opening in his head. After the surgeon examined Jay, he said, 'If he were my son, he'd be on the operating table tomorrow.' The immediacy of surgery shocked me. I had no time to mentally or emotionally prepare."

"What did the surgery involve?" I asked.

"Dr. Jones told us he'd have to saw through Jay's skull twice—side by side and an inch apart—from his forehead to the base of his skull." Loretta dragged her index finger like a scalpel over her head. "Then, he'd place plastic on the four sides of the bone to keep the skull from fusing together. This procedure would give him the necessary space for his brain to grow."

I shuddered as I tried to imagine the horror Loretta must have felt in that moment. Is there anything more terrifying than allowing your helpless baby to be cut apart?

Loretta fidgeted with the edge of her paper placemat. "Dr. Jones warned us this was a dangerous and complicated surgery for a five-month-old, but we had no choice. We signed the consent papers, and Dr. Jones scheduled surgery for the next morning."

I shook my head. "How does a baby survive that kind of invasive procedure?"

"I've no idea." The pitch in Loretta's voice rose with tension. "I could barely breathe as I watched the nurse wheel Jay away to the operating room. It was the hardest thing I'd ever done, to release him and not know if he'd come out alive. Much of that day is foggy, but I remember my emotions reached perilous heights as I waited for Jay to get out of surgery."

I listened, aware of the distress in Loretta's voice as she resurrected this moment of anguish. I knew Loretta was a woman with grit. But I could tell that motherhood was the area of her vulnerability, the place where she was most susceptible to the forces of fear. As one mom to another, I could relate.

"I tried to be calm and focus on God instead of my wild imagination leading up to that day. But, the gravity of someone sawing through Jay's skull was my undoing. I was a wreck."

"How did you get through it?"

"Lots and lots of prayer," she said. "And I was taking a college literature class at that time so I brought my textbook to the hospital to distract myself during Jay's surgery. Who knows how many times I read the same paragraph."

I chewed on the end of my wooden chopstick. I felt nervous for Loretta, as if I were waiting with her, anticipating the surgery's outcome.

"Brian and I decided to wait on a bench opposite the elevator where we knew Dr. Jones would come from the operating room. We'd tense every time the elevator door opened, hoping to see the surgeon emerge. After three hours, Dr. Jones walked out of the elevator and strolled towards us, wearing his green scrubs and a huge smile."

"Bearing good news?" I asked, hopefully.

She nodded. "I expected him to look exhausted, but he was animated and ecstatic. He told us, 'Jay fought through the surgery and everything went great.'"

I relaxed my shoulders and laid the chopstick down. "What an enormous relief."

"Jay had survived, and that's all that mattered to anyone that day. But, Dr. Jones also said a successful surgery did not guarantee a successful outcome. At a follow-up appointment, he told us there was a probable chance Jay would need more surgery when he turned two because that's when his brain would stop growing."

"Oh no!" I said. "I can't imagine how unnerving that must have been for you."

"Dr. Jones also said there was a 50/50 chance our son might have mental retardation. Nowadays, I think they use the term 'intellectual disabilities.' I only know that the odds he used made my skin crawl. I had difficulty concentrating as he explained that Jay would need weekly examinations and neurological tests to monitor his progress." Loretta's face crumpled. "Jay's prognosis felt as daunting as if Dr. Jones had told me to carry a boulder uphill."

"So how did you handle that news?"

Loretta sighed. "A low panic started in me and escalated over the next year. Instead of trusting God for Jay's health, I questioned him for allowing it to happen in the first place."

"So before Brian's death, you *did* question God?"

"Yes."

I rolled the tiny paper from my fortune cookie into a scroll, glad for her honesty.

"A few weeks after surgery, Jay came home. He grew. He seemed content. But when he showed no interest in rolling over like other babies his age, it scared me. My imagination was already in full throttle . . . racing out of control. I felt guilty and small minded, but my underlying fear—the thought that hounded me—was this. Did Jay have brain damage? And could I handle that?"

Loretta's shoulders sagged. "I'd fixate on Jay's motor skills and encourage him to roll over, sit up, and crawl. But I had no control over those things. I'd stay awake at night, my stomach churning, as I tried to picture what it'd look like if I had a disabled child. Would he be able to learn at all? How long would he live? Would I be able to rise to the task of caring for him?"

"I think any mom would ask those questions," I said.

Loretta straightened her shoulders.

"My need for control consumed me. A person can only live that away for so long. One afternoon I was exhausted from worry for Jay. I went outside for some fresh air and stood in my front yard. It was November. The Sweetgum's leaves had turned a brilliant yellow. Until that day, I'd been too distraught to notice the change of seasons. But that moment became a pivotal point in my life."

"Why? What happened?"

"As the sun bore down on me, I had to shield my eyes from its brightness. And I remember thinking I can continue to live on empty and make myself ill, or trust God with my son's well-being. I fell to my knees and cried, 'Father, I can't do this anymore. I release Jay to you. From now on, I choose to trust you . . . even in this!'"

Even in this reverberated in my mind. Were there areas that I refused to trust God even in this situation?

"Loretta, why is it so difficult to hand our kids over to God? I can trust God with my husband's job, where we live, and my health. But my kids? That has to be the greatest act of surrender."

"That decision to trust God radically changed me," Loretta said in a raspy, thick voice. "Over the next few years, I experienced God walking beside me step by step, one day at a time. That experience redefined my relationship with the Lord and paved the way for everything else in my life that would test my faith and love for him."

I swallowed hard, remembering my own surrender moments. "After you surrendered, did you ever try to take back control?"

"I was tempted, but I didn't. Who better to be in control than God? Even so, learning to trust God with unwavering confidence was like learning to walk. I had to take baby steps, one step at a time, every day. Sometimes, I acted flighty and doubtful, especially when we were at the hospital around children who were disabled. But I never sank to the same level of despair I'd felt before I surrendered Jay's welfare into God's hands."

Loretta's giant faith was built through baby steps of trust. Made sense to me. "What was Jay's final diagnosis?"

"Jay never needed another surgery. He was also blessed with a gifted mind and a head of red curls to cover those scars."

"And your other two children?" I asked. "Were they born healthy?"

"Would you believe they both had the same condition but not as extreme? Suffice to say, they're both healthy now."

I took a sip of my tepid tea. "When you offered to mentor me, I thought we'd have our nose in the Bible and discuss our faith. But your life—more than your words—shows me how to live by faith. I see your choices to trust God. I want to trust him like you do. What's wrong with me? Why can't I stop questioning God? Why can't I surrender what I can't control without engaging in a tug of war?"

"Don't be so hard on yourself. Walking by faith means taking baby steps. Over time, we learn to trust God more because he's proven himself in so many ways that we're finally able to trust completely."

Loretta squeezed my hand. "Don't worry. You'll get there. You're already getting there. Just keep walking, Karen. Faith is God's gift to you. Trusting God is what you do with that gift."

Take Away Nuggets

 Giant faith is built through baby steps of trust.

 "For we walk by faith, not by sight [living our lives in a manner consistent with our confident belief in God's promises]" (2 Corinthians 5:7 AMP).

Food for Thought

1. Recall a time when you challenged God by questioning his ways or his character. What underlying emotions and attitudes drove your questions? How did these emotions and attitudes impact your faith? Do you view this situation differently now that some time has passed? If so, how?

2. When Loretta's husband died, her faith in God remained firm because God had grown her faith through "baby steps" of trust in the preceding years. What baby steps of faith can you take in the coming days to fortify your own faith? Why are these baby steps important?

3. Do you believe God is the Absolute Controller of all things? How do you respond when you feel out of control? Both Karen and Loretta had moments in which they completely surrendered heartbreaking issues to God because they believed he was trustworthy. Is there something that keeps you from surrendering everything to him? If so, what is it and what would it take to remove this barrier?

CHAPTER 5

He Loves Me Not ...

To know that God knows everything about me and
yet loves me is indeed my ultimate consolation.
—R.C. Sproul

Clean, cool air swept through the front windows of my
minivan as I wound my way along the foothills to Loretta's
house. I glanced at my driving directions and veered right.
This was my first visit to her home. The way my insides wiggled
with anticipation, you'd think I'd received an invitation to meet
the Queen Mother. However, Loretta would yell "off with her
head," if she thought I placed her on a pedestal. "Don't think too
highly of me," she'd insist. I tried not to, but there were few people
who inspired me to seek a deeper relationship with the Lord the
way she did.

Loretta's single-story house sprawled on the middle of five acres.
My tires crunched on the gravel driveway as I drove past a dozen
bare-limbed saplings which stood like gangly soldiers guarding her

home. Bird feeders and chimes dangled from the wooden eaves of her front porch. As I slid from the car, Loretta came outside wearing a pair of blue jeans, a red turtleneck, and a welcoming smile. A cocker spaniel ambled stiffly towards me, sniffed my boots, and, seemingly satisfied, escorted me to his mistress.

"I see you've met Murph. Not a spring chicken, but he's a love," said Loretta, engulfing me in her arms. Her turtleneck smelled like toasted walnuts. "You want the nickel tour before we eat?"

Loretta held the door open and I walked inside. The tantalizing smell of baked goods greeted me as my eyes scanned the open floor plan where the living room flowed into the dining area. When we first met, I'd tried to imagine the type of home Loretta lived in based on what I knew about her. Because she had a magnetic aura of spirituality that drew people to her, I could easily picture her sitting by a stone hearth reading *My Utmost for His Highest* by Oswald Chambers. Or, strolling the halls of a stone convent with her hands clasped in prayer like Mother Superior. Not even close.

"I'm a regular joe," Loretta once told me. "I grew up in Iowa climbing trees, beating up boys, and running barefoot."

Her lack of pretense displayed itself in her warm, simple living room. An heirloom chest, an antique secretary desk displaying old memorabilia, and a coffee table made from a grape press reminded me of stepping into an Amish home. Two wooden end tables anchored her green couch and red chair. One of the end tables showcased several white-framed photos of her three grown children, their spouses, and seven grandchildren. Loretta matched names with faces. I felt an instant connection to these people I'd prayed for, but had yet to meet.

As I toured her three-bedroom home, Loretta described how she'd painted her bedroom walls and did handiwork around the house. A new image of Loretta emerged—a woman with Raw Silk paint smudged on her timeworn face, a hammer in one hand, a paintbrush in the other, and a row of nails gripped between her teeth.

When we came to the guest room, I pointed to a quilt on the bed. "Where'd you get that? It's lovely."

"It belonged to my maternal grandma. I first slept under it when I was eight years old. I love seeing the fabrics that were her dresses and aprons. The hexagonal pattern is called Grandmother's Flower Garden." Loretta stroked the yellow scalloped edge with the same degree of tenderness with which she might have caressed her grandma's face.

I pointed to an older couple in a black and white photograph on her antique dresser. "Are these your grandparents?"

"Yes, they lived on a farm. It was probably my favorite place in the world." Loretta picked up a framed newspaper clipping that had yellowed with age. "And the couple in this photo are my parents. They were ballroom dance instructors known as the Debonairs. I remember watching them dance throughout the house." Loretta swiped her thumb across the glass to brush away a thin film of dust. "That was before—"

I waited for her to finish her statement, but she quickly changed the subject. "Ready to eat?" she asked.

I followed Loretta into the heat of the kitchen, wondering what she'd failed to mention. She dished up two steaming bowls of French onion soup, piled on a thick layer of Gruyere cheese, and set them on the oak dining table. We settled in and held hands.

"Merciful, sweet Father," Loretta prayed, "we thank you for all you've done for us. For your love demonstrated on the cross and your faithfulness. We love you and want to please you with our lives." Loretta squeezed my hands. Her voice softened. "I lift up my friend, Karen. Be all that she needs today. We thank you for this food, and pray your Spirit will nourish our souls. Amen."

I swallowed a lump in the back of my throat and looked at Loretta. The woman was velvet over steel—soft in heart when she spoke of God, or of me, and yet iron-strong in her approach to life.

"You amaze me, Loretta. You're my mentor. A handyman. A part-time bookkeeper. Is there anything you can't do?"

"I'm not a great cook." She grinned and picked up her soup spoon. "But, after Brian died, I had to be on a strict budget. I learned to do most things myself rather than pay someone else to do them." She tucked a white strand of hair behind her ear. "Besides, I'm also the first-born child of no-nonsense parents. I inherited my mother's German can-do mentality and work ethic. My hardest task in life is asking others for help, especially from my grown children."

"I know the feeling," I said. "My paternal Texan roots run deep. I pitch in when someone needs help, but it's difficult to accept help." I blew on my spoonful of soup to cool it down. "But I think my hardest task in life is believing that God loves me—all the time. I try to do the right thing and be a good person, but I fail way too often. And when that happens, I wonder how he feels about me."

"That's not unusual," she replied. "I think a lot of women struggle with feeling that God truly loves them."

"Do you ever feel that way?"

"I struggle with many things, but knowing that God loves me isn't one of them. I can't explain it. I only know God loves me today as much as he did yesterday."

I looked into Loretta's calm eyes and sighed. "I wish I had your confidence, but it's just hard to believe his love for me doesn't vary from day to day."

"Are you saying you think God loves you less when you do something bad?"

I shrugged. "Doesn't have to be bad. Sometimes, it's what I *don't do*. I skipped my morning prayers last week. I didn't volunteer to help in children's Sunday School even though they desperately needed it. I didn't share the gospel with my neighbor when I had the opportunity. So it seems like God would love me less than he did two weeks ago when I prayed every morning for over an hour, made dinner for a sick friend, and had bedtime devotions with Jason."

Loretta raised her brows. "Weird Margaret. I'm thankful God's love doesn't depend on our actions or we'd all be in a fix."

Loretta's silly phrase made me laugh at myself. I guess my words *did* sound weird. And yet, I couldn't dismiss the doubts that gnawed like termites at the foundation of my faith.

"Loretta, I know in my *head* that God loves me, but sometimes I can't get my *heart* to believe it. I can't help but think that God gets mad at me when I'm indifferent toward him. Or when I fail to do what I know he wants me to do."

A puzzled expression crossed Loretta's face.

I gestured with my chin. "Don't you ever wonder if God's mad at you?"

"I've felt guilty plenty of times. And I've told God I'm sorry," she replied. "But I never thought he was *mad* at me."

"Okay, maybe frustrated is a better word. Do you ever picture God rolling his eyes at you whenever you mess up?"

"Shoot bother." She sighed. "I mess up every day. Doesn't mean God's mad."

I wiped a string of melted cheese from my lip, then put down my spoon and voiced my thoughts. "Okay, I'm just being honest here, and the best way I can describe this is what happened with my kids this past week. I love those kids like crazy. I constantly bend over backwards for them. I do everything in my power to make them happy and meet their needs. I'd die for them. But, at times I found myself rolling my eyes...."

Loretta stifled a smile as my eyes bulged and circled like two billiard balls.

"And it wasn't because they did something bad," I continued. "It was what they *didn't* do that frustrated me. Like not unloading the dishwasher or cleaning the cat's litter box, unless I made a ruckus. They also acted ungrateful when I helped them with their homework. I still love them, but, frankly, I don't feel as *loving* toward them. So why shouldn't God feel that way toward me when I'm being a brat?"

Loretta stared thoughtfully at her soup.

Oh no, what is she thinking? She probably thinks I'm a horrible mom. And a horrible Christian. I wanted to crawl under the table with Murph.

"You're right, Karen," Loretta said tenderly with no speck of judgement in her voice. "When we use human experiences to explain God's love for us, we come up short."

Mercy, how I loved this woman.

"But, we're flawed and God is not," she added. "God's love for us is so much more complete and purer than we can possibly understand." Loretta pointed to the framed photos of her family on the end table. "I think the closest human experience we have to show God's love is giving birth. Remember when your children were born? You loved them, right?"

"More than I'd ever thought possible," I replied.

"And yet, they'd done nothing to earn your love except to be present."

"True." I thought of Jonathan, my first-born. I remembered sitting in the hospital bed studying his tiny fingernails and sweet face. As I did, an unexplainable, consuming love for him filled every fiber of my being. I could still feel the force, the purity, the power of that love. Nothing Jonathan did—or didn't do—had ever kept me from loving him. Oh yes, this was the love of God. I needed to see myself this way, a babe in God's arms with his deep love pouring out on me with unshakable force. Certainly I'd had glimpses of God's perfect love for me . . . but I couldn't seem to *keep* my heart in that place.

Loretta reached for a white pitcher on the table and poured a stream of cool, refreshing water into my glass. I suddenly felt parched. How could I be a Christian for decades and still feel so thirsty for God's love? I took a few sips and set my glass down.

"Two weeks ago," I said, "I had an epiphany—one of those God moments—that curled my toes."

Loretta leaned forward. "Tell me. What happened?"

"I woke up early and went outside to pray. A brilliant burnt-orange sun crept above the foothills and bathed the pine trees in my yard in gold. The way their limbs swayed in the breeze made me think of an angel choir lifting their arms to heaven. It took my breath away."

Loretta smiled.

"I wanted to praise God for his beautiful creation and experience the joy of his presence. So I started singing, "Jesus Loves Me." Loretta, I felt such joy in that moment that I can hardly describe it. But then, out of nowhere, a harsh voice came into my head. I knew it wasn't God's voice because it was very accusing. It said, 'Do you *know* Jesus loves you? Because *you don't live like you believe it.* You act like you have to be perfect for God to love you.'"

"Ooh, that must have sent shivers down your spine."

"It jarred me. Even so, that snarly voice was spot on. I know God loves me. I can point to Romans 8:38 and 39 that says nothing can separate me from his love. But for some reason, my heart struggles to believe God would love me that much."

Tears blurred my vision.

"Karen, why are you so hard on yourself?"

I ran my hand over the oak table, feeling its rough grain. How could I explain a lifetime of never feeling good enough, or able to do enough, to deserve God's love?

My throat caught, and for a moment I thought I might not be able to speak. "Who knows? Maybe that's how I'm wired."

Loretta frowned.

"I know that's negative self-talk," I said in my defense. "My inner critic won't let me get away with anything."

"Could be," Loretta said. "Or maybe it's the voice of our Enemy, Satan, that keeps you from trusting God's love. He loves to torment our minds and keep us in a place of doubt."

"Really? Satan?" I said doubtfully. I believed what the Bible said about him, that he was the leader of an army of dark spirits. But I figured he had more important things to do than to bother with little ole' me.

"Bottom line," she said, tapping the table with her spoon. "The Enemy will accuse and remind you of wrongdoing which leads to shame and fear. Unlike God's Spirit, who convicts us to stop doing things that hurt ourselves or others. Shame and condemnation are never from God."

"Let me get this straight. You think the reason I doubt God's love for me is because I'm listening to the voice of Satan?"

"Possibly. Or it could be because you are hearing voices from your past. You know, those hurtful things others say about us that stick to us like nettles in our socks. You know the kind of voices I mean."

I did.

"But, let me ask you something."

"Sure."

"Do you think it might be possible to know—to know beyond a shadow of doubt—that God loves you even if you don't trust him?"

"You really like the word 'trust,' don't you? You bring it up all the time."

"That's because I believe with all my heart that *trusting God* is the most important ingredient in a believer's life." She waved her spoon in the air as if to say, *listen* up. "If you want to rest in God's love, it begins with trusting God when he says, 'I love you.'"

I put my elbows on the table, folded my hands together, and thought of Dan. We said, "I love you," every day—at bedtime, when he left on a trip, when we talked long-distance on the phone, and when we texted. The words came easily. I believed Dan. I had no reason to doubt his love. He'd shown me love in countless ways. But could I honestly say I trusted him to be faithful and love me forever? Not really, and through no fault of his own.

From the day we got married, I'd struggled with feeling secure in his love. Two days into the honeymoon I'd teased him, "Are you glad you married me? Do you still love me?" Twenty years into our marriage, if we had an argument that kept us from speaking all day, I'd wonder if Dan's love had limits. I'd worry he'd stop loving me.

Where did those insecurities come from? I hadn't a clue. I only knew they were there. And they were a huge factor in my ability to trust God's love for me.

Loretta touched my arm, interrupting my thoughts. "Karen, do you want to know for certain that God's love for you is eternal and unwavering?"

My eyes grew wide. "Absolutely."

"Then you must *know* God's character. When I was in my forties, God got my attention when I read Exodus 33:13. Moses is desperate and asks one thing of God. 'Let me know your ways so I may understand you more fully.' That became my focus and goal—to know God. For three years, I spent all my spare time searching God's Word, Genesis and Exodus in particular, to learn about his character . . . who he was, along with how and why he interacted with his people.

"Every time I read my Bible I took a pen and drew a heart near every action that showed God's character—like pursuing. Now, when I open my Bible, I see those hearts littered in the margins and I'm reminded who God is. His characteristics pop out at me."

"I like that." I smiled. "You could also draw hearts by descriptive words like 'kind' and 'patient'?"

"You could." She nodded. "If you only look for God's judgement and wrath in the Old Testament, you'll find it. But as I marked his actions, what stood out was how forgiving and merciful he was to such disobedient children because he loved them."

Loretta leaned back and folded her arms across her lap. "I can't say it enough. Knowing God's character helped me see him in a whole new way. As A.W. Tozer says, 'What comes into our minds when we think about God is the most important thing about us.'"

"I love that thought," I said, wishing I had a pen and paper to jot it down. *What comes into our minds ... what comes into* my *mind ... when I think about God?*

Before I could make a mental inventory, Loretta added. "Just remember, Karen, it's not enough to highlight God's characteristics. We have to *believe* they're true. Otherwise we won't trust God's love when we're going through tough times. Or when we fail."

Her voice softened as she searched my eyes. "And why not trust him?"

Why not? You mean what "keeps me" from trusting a God who is perfectly trustworthy? I blinked back tears. I didn't have an answer. But I knew a two-hour lunch with Loretta wasn't going to change me. Some faith lessons can't be wrapped in wax paper like a sandwich and tied with a string.

Loretta stood, gathered our soup bowls, and took them to the kitchen. Then she returned with a plate of heart-shaped scones and set them in front of me.

Screech. Screech. Murph pawed the front door.

"Poor Murph," Loretta cooed. "Do you need to go out?"

She hurried towards him, and then glanced back at me after she opened the door and stepped outside. "I'll just be a second. Help yourself to a scone. Made them myself. I used apricots, white chocolate, and toasted walnuts."

"And you said you weren't a good cook," I mumbled, eyeing the mouthwatering dessert.

However, I wanted more than a momentary sugar high. I wanted what Loretta had—sweet fellowship with the Lord that allowed his love to gush out of her heart like the bits of dried apricots peeking through the surface of these warm scones. What did I need to do to taste and experience God's love?

Take Away Nuggets

 God's love for you is eternal and unwavering.

 I am convinced that nothing can ever separate us from God's love . . . not even the powers of hell can separate us from God's love (Romans 8:38).

Food for
Thought

1. Do accusing voices in your head try to convince you that you aren't worthy of God's love—or that God loves you less—when you aren't at your best? Where do those voices come from? What can you do to silence them and trust God's love for you?

2. According to Romans 8:38-39, what can separate you from God's love? Commit these powerful verses to memory.

3. Loretta says that knowing God's character is an integral part of our ability to trust him. What have you done to get to know God's character? List ten of God's attributes and consider how those qualities impact you.

4. How has God demonstrated his love for you in the past? Spend a few moments now thanking him for the riches of his love displayed to you.

CHAPTER **6**

He Loves Me

God loves each of us as if there was only one of us.
—St Augustine

*L*oretta was still outside with Murph. I took a heart-shaped scone from the platter and broke it in two. I devoured one half and left the other half on the platter. Part of my heart believed that God loved me the same all the time, another part doubted. Was it because I kept listening to the negative voices in my head that told me I wasn't worthy of such love? Was it because I doubted God? Or, was there something in my past that blocked me from receiving God's love? Would I ever find the answer?

Wham! A strong breeze shoved the door open and interrupted my musing. Loretta entered with Murph at her heels, panting like he'd just climbed Mt. Everest.

"Sorry about that," Loretta said as she slid into her seat at the table. She picked up the platter of scones and offered them to me. A smile flickered across her face when she noticed part of one scone was already missing. She took a scone for herself and set it on her dessert plate.

"Karen, have I told you about my younger brother, Russell?"

This was an abrupt change in subject from what we'd been discussing. I leaned in, sensing that whatever Loretta was about to say was important.

"I don't think so," I replied. "You mentioned once that you have a younger brother and sister."

"I do. But Russell died before they were born."

Her words took me by surprise. "Oh, I'm sorry. When did it happen?"

"I was fourteen when Russell died. He was eleven." Loretta inhaled and let her breath out slowly. I watched her body stiffen slightly. A far-away look filled her tender eyes as she slipped back in time.

"It was a Saturday afternoon. I wanted to make cream puffs for my family because I'd learned to make them in home economics the week before. I'd already started making the pastry when I realized we were out of milk, so I asked Russell to go to the store and get some. The store was only a few blocks away . . . " Murph walked over and sat by Loretta's feet. She patted him on the head.

"Russell was gone a long time. At first I was annoyed because he was holding up my baking project. I tried to imagine why he hadn't returned—maybe he'd stopped at a friend's house. But as the minutes passed, I grew more anxious."

As I listened, my stomach dropped, remembering the tortuous hours Loretta had waited for Brian to return home from his ill-fated flight.

"Finally, around 4:30, the door burst open. I ran to it, expecting to see Russell, but it was my dad. I took one look at his dazed eyes and slumped shoulders and knew that something terrible had happened. Dad fell into his chair and started bawling. I had to piece the events together because he was sobbing so hard he could barely speak."

Loretta leaned down, stroking Murph's back. "Evidently, Dad had been driving home from work when he'd spotted a police car and several people gathered in the middle of the road. He'd pulled over to see if he could help. Someone told him that a boy had been crossing the street when he'd been hit by a car. The driver hadn't seen him because the sun was in his eyes. When Dad saw the lifeless form on the ground, he panicked. He couldn't see the boy's face, but a parent knows his own flesh and blood."

Loretta's hand went to her throat and she momentarily closed her eyes as though she had to summon the words to come out.

"Dad shoved his way past the police officer and knelt beside Russell in a puddle of spilled milk. Shards of glass from the broken milk bottle clung to my brother's ashen face and were embedded in his hair like ice crystals. Dad picked off the glass as best he could. Then he stumbled to his car and grabbed a blanket to drape over Russell."

A blanket, I thought. A desperate father's longing to keep his son warm and safe until the ambulance arrived. I wondered, had a scream boiled up in his throat? Had he held Russell's limp, crushed body to his chest, trying to hug the life back into him? To even think of the death of a child sent electricity tingling through my spine. *What if that had happened to one of my kids?*

But it wasn't one of my kids who'd taken their last breath when cold steel and screeching tires had slammed into human flesh. It was Loretta's brother. A youth on a simple errand—who never returned home.

Loretta's lips tightened into a thin line. "Russell's death horrified me. I couldn't even cry. I just went numb. In fact, I don't remember anything else that happened that evening except seeing my six-foot-five, stoic dad weep like a child. I'd never seen him cry. I felt helpless to do anything to make him stop crying. Then a horrendous thought came into my mind. *If I hadn't made Russell go to the store, he would still be alive. Dad's heartache, Russell's death . . . it's all my fault."*

Loretta rubbed her brow. I wondered how many times she'd tried to erase that heart-wrenching memory.

"I never told my parents that I blamed myself for Russell's death. I didn't know how."

"Did your parents blame you?"

"No. My dad said some cruel things to me when I was a child, but he never accused me of Russell's death." Loretta's eyes darkened. "But, they also didn't ask me how I felt about what happened. You see, Russell died in 1951. People were less vocal about their feelings back then. Our family never talked about our emotions. There were never any hugs. My parents didn't even ask me about my day when we ate supper together."

I shook my head emphatically. I couldn't imagine living like that. My folks had been affectionate and engaged with me my whole life.

"That's why I missed Russell so much," Loretta explained. "We slept in the same room. We'd lay awake at night and jabber about our friends, laugh about our favorite hiding places for Hide and Seek, and make plans to build a fort until Dad would holler from the next room, 'Enough! Go to sleep.'

"Russell and I got on so well, which was a bit of a surprise since we were polar opposites in many ways. I was gregarious like Dad. Russell took after our mom, who was quiet and melancholy. Plus, when my brother was young, he'd had scarlet fever which left him physically weak. I considered myself his protector."

Loretta paused. Her gaze veered past me and out the dining room window. In her mind's eye, did she see the rustling cornfields of Iowa where she'd grown up instead of the California foothills? And then she looked at me with an impish smile.

"I'll never forget the day Russell ran into the house with tears streaming down his face. His cheek was red and swollen. A boy his age—he was nine at the time—had hit him. I told Russell I'd take care of it. Nobody was going to bully my little brother. I made a beeline for that boy's house. But when I knocked on the door, the kid's older brother, Ronnie, answered. He was thirteen, a year older than me, and a head taller. But I didn't back down. We stood toe to toe. I ranted about his brother's unacceptable behavior. Ronnie shrugged and mumbled something like, 'Who cares.' Talk about seeing red. I clenched my fist, pulled back my arm, and popped him in the face."

"You're joking, right?"

"Didn't think twice." She slapped the table like a judge with a gavel. "Ronnie's jaw dropped and, to his credit, he punched me right back. Didn't matter that I was a girl. I was the leader of the neighborhood pack and had a reputation for beating up boys. Unfortunately, that reputation came at a price." Loretta traced the left side of her long nose with her index finger. "I still have a small bump where Ronnie hit me and I can hardly breathe out of that nostril."

I stifled a giggle. Apparently there were many things I didn't know about my mentor. "I can't believe you started a fist fight. But kudos to you for trying to protect your little brother."

Loretta's face went somber. "But in the end, I *didn't* protect him."

My heart ached for my friend. *Some things are simply beyond our control.*

"After Russell's death, our home became a tomb—dark and silent. I felt invisible. I had no one to talk to about my feelings so I simply stuffed them in an effort to block the pain."

I fumbled for something to say. "Did you try talking to God?"

"No. Our family didn't go to church then so I rarely thought about God. But, both my mom and Russell had a relationship with

Jesus. Mom used to listen to preachers on the radio, and sometimes I'd catch bits of their messages. Other than God's bigness, I didn't know much about him."

"When did that change?" I pressed, eager to know my mentor's spiritual journey.

"A month after Russell died, one of dad's co-workers invited our family to go to his church. I sat with my parents on a wooden pew, trying not to focus on the empty space beside me where Russell would have sat. The pastor started talking about a verse in the Bible, Romans 6:23. Perhaps other people heard him say, 'For the wages of sin is death, but the free gift of God is eternal life through Christ Jesus our Lord.' But what I heard in my fourteen-year-old heart was this: God sees me. He knows my name. He loves me!"

Loretta took off her glasses and blotted her wet cheeks with her shirt sleeve. "Karen, I remember thinking, here sits a girl whose brother died because she sent him to the store. A girl who has horrible acne. A girl who has short, permed hair that makes her look matronly. A girl others call 'String Bean' because she's five feet nine and skinny. A girl whose father calls her 'featherbrain.' But honestly, in that moment, none of that mattered. God saw my pimples. He knew others made fun of me. He knew about Russell. And yet, he still loved me. Little ol' me, Loretta Jean."

I studied Loretta's face like an artist studies the object of her inspiration. The more she talked about meeting God, the brighter her face shone.

"It was more than my young heart could comprehend," she continued. "I'd always thought of myself as a happy child, but when God introduced himself to me that day, I experienced a new joy that sent me over the moon! I jumped in with both feet. I joined the church youth group and started reading my Bible. Over time, any guilt I felt about me being responsible for Russell's death was replaced by God's inexplicable peace. What a gift! It still scrambles my eggs!"

Loretta took a bite of her scone. I suspect she thought the story was over, but I wanted to hear more. How was it that Loretta had grown up in a home where love was rarely demonstrated, and yet she felt secure in God's love for her while I'd grown up with parents who told me they loved me, but I struggled to receive his love? It didn't make sense.

I put my unspoken thoughts on the table.

"Loretta, you mentioned that your dad wasn't affectionate, that he didn't try to connect emotionally with you. I've heard that people who have abusive or absent fathers find it more difficult to accept God's love. Do you agree?"

"I've heard the same thing, but that wasn't my case. A lack of love in my home actually made me more eager for God because I so desperately needed to be loved." Loretta scraped the scone crumbs that were lying on her placemat into her hand, and dumped them on her plate. "My dad was a hardworking, outgoing man who could laugh at himself. But I never felt loved by him. I'll never forget Dad saying, 'Loretta, come here. I have something to tell you.' I walked over to the couch where he sat and stood in front of him, my heart pounding with excitement because Dad actually had a message for me. He looked me in the eyes and told me matter-of-factly, 'Loretta, you're ugly, you're dirty, and you have no friends. If you think you do, you're deceiving yourself.'"

I gasped. "That's a horrible, appalling thing to say!"

She drew a deep breath and for a second I thought she'd cry.

"How old were you when this happened?"

"Ten. I wish I could tell you that it only happened once, but Dad said the same thing repeatedly throughout my adolescent years."

"That's cruel," I snapped. "Why would he say that to you?"

"I confronted my dad with that same question when I was forty-two, shortly before he died. We were sitting at the kitchen table when I told him, 'Dad, your words almost killed me.' He leaned forward and tapped the table with his finger. 'Loretta, you're the person you are today because I said those words. Whenever I pushed you down, you got above it.'"

"Oh, Loretta," I groaned. "So your dad thought he'd strengthened your character by saying those things. What did you say to him?"

"I said, 'No, Dad, I am who I am today because I needed to be loved so much that I ran to God.'" Loretta slowly shook her head. "I can't hate Dad. His words led me to an intense relationship with my Father God. But it hurts that my dad never apologized for the way he spoke to me during those impressionable, childhood years. And he died without ever telling me what I wanted to hear . . . "

Neither one of us finished her sentence. "I love you" hung in the air between us.

Murphy must have sensed Loretta's sorrow. He stood on his hind legs with his front paws on her thigh, waving his tail as if to say, "Don't be sad. I'm here."

"For crying me a bucket!" Loretta tousled the fur on Murph's head. "Aren't we a pair?"

I watched the two of them love on each other, but my insides agitated when I thought about Loretta's dad. How many years had it been? Decades? And she still remembered his cruel words. They were written on her heart the same as if he'd scrawled "ugly," "dirty," "friendless" with indelible ink on her bedroom wall.

I wanted to erase her dad's remarks, to alleviate her pain. But what could I say? I'd never stood in Loretta's shoes in front of that couch in Iowa. My own dad always ended every conversation we had with those three words that every daughter needed to hear . . . "I love you."

I braced both hands around my water glass. "Loretta, may I ask you something personal?"

She nodded.

"Were the loving words God spoke to you after Russell's death enough to cancel out your father's negative words? Or do you still hear your dad's voice in your head? I only ask because we were talking earlier about negative voices and how to deal with them."

Loretta's forehead wrinkled as if puzzling through my question. "When my dad said those things to me, I believed they were true. I felt ugly. My permed hair, my acne, and my height, confirmed his indictment. But that day in church changed everything. It's hard to explain, but it's as if my dad's words no longer had any authority over me. God was now my father. He was my authority. I needed to listen and believe his words to me, not my dad's."

She took a sip of water. "You know, we can't remove the negative voices in our heads once we've heard them, but we can mute them. And replace them with the powerful, positive words that God speaks to us."

I nodded, glad Loretta knew which voice to listen to, but I couldn't handle any more words. My stuffed brain was about to burst. I reached for the lonely broken scone on the platter, broke it in half again, and slipped a bite into my mouth. Only this time, I chewed slowly and allowed my taste buds to enjoy the diced apricots. Their faint tartness, combined with the sweet white chocolate, danced inside my mouth. "Loretta, these scones are heavenly."

"Would you like another?" Loretta asked.

"No, you already gave me enough to chew on," I said playfully. I checked my phone and quickly pushed my chair back from the table. "I hate to leave, but I need to get Jason from school."

"Wait," Loretta said. "I have something for you."

Before I could leave, Loretta gave me a plastic bag of scones. Then, she hugged me tighter than normal and said, "Karen, God loves you like no human can. He has a purpose for your life that exceeds anything your mind or heart can conceive. Is that someone you can trust?"

I headed for my car. Full hands. Full tummy. Full heart. Loretta had fed me well.

∽

In the weeks that followed, I thought often about our conversation. I loved how God had assured Loretta that he'd known her name and he accepted her as faultless. Somehow she'd refused to allow her dad's words to define her, and had chosen instead to believe who she was in Christ—that she was beautiful and loved.

And then there was me. Unlike Loretta, I'd grown up with a dad who loved me unconditionally. So why did I still feel like God's love for me depended on my efforts?

Loretta had suggested that I was hard on myself, that I was listening to the wrong voices. Was she right?

On one of my morning walks, one of those negative voices chided me, "Karen, how many times can you disappoint God and expect him to love you?" Something flipped inside of me and I got mad. Mad that I'd wasted years listening to Satan's lies instead of God's love-filled promises. Mad at myself, for allowing my inner critic to put me down.

I clenched my fists. *Stop it! I'm not listening anymore to these lies!* In that moment, I vowed to go toe to toe with those bully voices and punch them out just like Loretta had hit that guy to defend her brother. I pledged to slay them, silence them.

From then on I did four things that helped me shut my ears to the negative voices and open my ears to God's voice.

I memorized verses that spoke of God's love for me. There are hundreds of Bible verses that speak of God's unending love, but two of my favorite were these: Romans 5:8 which declares, "God showed his great love for us by sending Christ to die for us while we were still sinners." And 1 John 4:9-10 which says, "God showed how much he loved us by sending his one and only Son into the world so that we might have eternal life through him. This is real love—not that we loved God, but that he loved us and sent his Son as a sacrifice to take away our sins."

I drew hearts next to God's characteristics and actions in the Bible that revealed his love. As I read Scripture through love-tinted lenses, God's love seemed wider and deeper. My Bible began to resemble a Valentine's card similar to those heart-shaped candies imprinted with the words I Love You. Be Mine. Forever Yours.

I read books that affirmed God's love for me such as Francine Rivers' *Redeeming Love*, Henri J. M. Nouwen's *The Return of The Prodigal Son*, and Brennan Manning's *The Ragamuffin Gospel*. I particularly loved this quote from Manning's book. "I could more easily contain Niagara Falls in a teacup than I can comprehend the wild, uncontainable love of God."

I prayed for God to show me his love in tangible ways. Each day I searched for God's love as though I was on a scavenger hunt. One day, God's tangible love arrived as a homemade lasagna made by my neighbor when I was ill. Another day, I was blown away when I went to my mailbox and found a note of encouragement from someone I barely knew. The perfect timing of that card (after a rough week) had God's fingerprints all over it.

The more I searched for God's love, the more I heard him singing me a love song at every turn. He said, "I love you" through my husband's intimate hugs. Through the love of family and friends who accepted me. Through the Sierra Nevadas' breathtaking vistas, the Big Dipper winking at me in the dark, and birds trilling a morning love ballad.

And then a loud "I love you" came from God in an unsuspecting moment.

My eight-year-old son had the flu. It was late at night when I heard Jason call out. I hurried to his bedroom and found him moaning in his sleep. I placed my hand on his clammy brow. His fever had broken.

"Lord," I prayed, "I can't stand it when my child suffers. I don't know how you could watch your Son die on the cross." Like a northern breeze murmuring through the trees, God whispered, **That's because you don't know how much I love you.**

Tears came. *Lord, I'm trying to understand. Help me.*

Jason sighed and rolled over on his side. I crawled beneath the covers and snuggled against him. His body relaxed. I couldn't comprehend God's love for me anymore than Jason could possibly understand how much I loved him. But I was trying. And I somehow knew the pursuit of this was the most important thing I could do because knowing, *really knowing* God's love, changes everything.

Take Away Nuggets

Your identity is not based on the opinion of others, but on God's radical love for you.

"But you, O Lord, are a God of compassion and mercy, slow to get angry and filled with unfailing love and faithfulness" (Psalm 86:15).

Food for Thought

1. Loretta said she believed her dad's cruel words until God became the new authority in her life. Whose words have authority in your life? What do you think God would want you to do so that his words have more authority over you?

2. Do you believe God sees you and loves you? If not, why not? How does knowing God loves you with an everlasting love change everything?

3. Karen mentioned four practical things she did to experience more of God's love. What is something you can begin doing today so you too know the deep and expansive love of God?

CHAPTER 7

The Question of Pain

It seems sometimes that there is no way to God's
Best but through pain, and yet how earnestly
one longs to save a dear one from it.
—Amy Carmichael, missionary

Three months slipped by between lunches with Loretta. My spirit felt as parched as California's golden foothills when I called her on a sizzling summer day to schedule a lunch date. I needed time with my spiritual mentor who kept me God-focused. I never considered that Loretta might need me.

"I can't drive to meet you for lunch," she said in a weak voice. "I pulled a back muscle trying to push my riding mower over a hump in the yard. I can barely walk."

"Oh no!" I replied. "Can I bring you some groceries? Clean your house?"

Her voice perked up. "That's not necessary, but I've missed you. Why don't you come to my house? Are you free tomorrow?"

"What time?"

"After lunch. Around one o'clock?"

"I'll be there!"

The next afternoon, I pulled into Loretta's sun-bleached gravel driveway. The last time I'd been to her home, we'd talked about God's love. Today, I had no agenda, no expectations. I just wanted to love on my friend who was in pain. I brought a chicken broccoli casserole and a picnic basket filled with angel food mini cakes, a pint of fresh strawberries, and a can of whipped cream. Hands bearing gifts of food, I walked to her front door and tapped it with the edge of my sandal.

"Door's unlocked," she hollered.

Loretta lay on her green plaid couch with an ice pack beneath her back and a box of tissues on her lap. She wore jeans and a striped knit shirt.

"I thought we'd decided to skip lunch," Loretta said as she spied the bundles in my arms.

"This is dinner. Eat at your own risk," I teased.

"Weird Margaret," she sighed. "Smells wonderful."

Loretta's cocker spaniel, Murph, sniffed the air and followed me into the kitchen. He sat on his haunches and swiped his tongue over his lips. "Sorry old fellow, this isn't for you." I set the casserole dish on the Formica counter and unpacked the basket. No dirty dishes in the sink. Everything in its place. Loretta was organized even when she felt poorly. But I knew, by the heaviness in her voice, that more was afoot than a bad back. Something else was troubling her. What?

I poked my head into the living room and called, "Loretta, can I get you something?"

"No, but please help yourself to the lemonade in the frig. And bring that package of dark chocolate pomegranates by the sink."

I returned with my lemonade and the sweet treats. Then I sat in the red recliner next to the couch and plopped several chocolates into my mouth. "Oh Loretta," I moaned, "these are out-of-this-world scrumptious." I grabbed another handful. "Changing the subject, how's my sweet friend?"

Loretta winced as she shifted positions to get a better look at me. Tears rimmed her eyes.

"I received a shocking phone call this morning. Phyllis, one of my dearest friends in the world—I've known her for more than forty years—died yesterday of a brain aneurism."

"Oh, Loretta, I'm so sorry!"

Loretta yanked a tissue from the box on her lap and wiped her wet cheeks. "I didn't even get to tell her goodbye."

I waited for Loretta to gather her emotions while I searched for words. But what could I say that would comfort my friend? With her grief so fresh, I needed to simply be present instead of sounding wise, and be okay with it. I needed to listen while Loretta choked back tears and talked about her friend.

"Phyllis was four years younger than me, but she knew spiritual things that I didn't. Her insight about God, the way she spoke, the way she carried herself . . . were wrapped in a quiet spirit. Phyllis sought God with focused determination. That's why I felt drawn to her. We could talk about God for hours." Loretta removed her glasses and rubbed the bridge of her nose. "I remember going to the beach with her years ago. We sat on a blanket and talked about intimacy with God and what that looked like in our lives. She told me, 'Life with God is a *process*.' It was a timely word. One that I needed to hear."

I nodded when Loretta mentioned the word "process." I already knew there wasn't a short cut to spiritual maturity. When my children were little, I wrongly presumed that if I was a good role model and trained them to follow Jesus, I could hasten their faith. But a person's faith can't be microwaved like popcorn. I only had to look at my own life to see that truth.

"Sounds like you and Phyllis were kindred spirits. How'd you meet?"

"We met through her parents. I don't know what they saw in Brian and me. We were poor seminary students, but they took us under their wings. Dr. Hotchkiss, who was a highly respected theology professor, developed a deep friendship with Brian. And Mrs. Hotchkiss became my spiritual mentor and treated me like one of her own. She even volunteered to make my wedding dress."

"Whoah, a wedding dress? Talk about a labor of love." I cocked my elbow on the arm of the recliner and rested my chin in my hand. "Give me details. What did it look like?"

"My dress was a stunning champagne peau de soie. It was knee-length with slender lines and sleeves just above the elbow. A classic Audrey Hepburn style."

I smiled and imagined Loretta swathed in elegance, gracefully floating down the aisle to meet her eager groom.

"Did I tell you that Brian is buried next to Dr. Hotchkiss?"

I shook my head.

"Dr. Hotchkiss passed away in January 1972. When Brian died ten months later, Mrs. Hotchkiss gave her burial plot to Brian because she knew how much they cared for each other." Loretta grabbed another tissue. "So you see, the loss of Phyllis goes deep because she and her parents were more like family. Now they're all gone."

"You obviously loved Phyllis a great deal. It must be very hard for you."

Loretta put her glasses back on. "Very hard, but pain is often the avenue that God uses in our lives to teach and change us. I can live with the pain as long as I can learn something from it."

Her answer didn't surprise me. How many times had Loretta told me she wanted God to teach and change her? More than I could count.

"Pain is a difficult teacher," I said, "but I'm not sure I want to sign up for a course with that instructor. Given the choice, I'd rather learn by hearing what God has taught you than to learn through my own pain."

Loretta laughed softly at my jest which brought a spasm of pain. She squeezed her eyes shut and then relaxed. "I don't blame you. But suffering provides an opportunity for God to work. So I've learned to submit to whatever happens and have a teachable heart because I know God is able to use this for my good. Even now, I'm willing to learn, but I'm struggling. I don't sleep well when I'm in pain. Between the back pain, the fatigue, and now Phyllis' death . . . I've got nothing. Even the joy of the Lord can be difficult to come by when you're living on empty."

I shifted in my chair. I'd never seen Loretta so frail. Flat on her back. Face strained; hair askew. I went to Loretta, knelt beside her, and held her hand. I asked God to heal and comfort her. To lift her spirits. To restore her joy. When I finished, Loretta locked eyes with me and whispered, "You're a gift to me."

I squeezed her hand and returned to my chair. For a few moments, the only sound in the room came from the low hum of the ceiling fan. Loretta's eyes were closed, but I knew she wasn't asleep. She was thinking, or praying.

"I'll get through this." She sighed. "I've been through harder things. Like 1973, which was the worst year of my life."

"Wait a minute. I thought Brian died in 1972?" I assumed his death would have been her worst year.

"He did. But the following year . . . while I was grieving for Brian and trying to grasp my new reality . . . three of my immediate family members died."

My mouth fell open. "Whaaat?"

She nodded. "My grandma, my mom's mom—the one who made the quilt on my guest bed—was a strict woman. Seldom laughed. But she knew how to make me smile. She always had Butter Brickle ice cream and tapioca pudding waiting for me whenever I'd visit. Anyway, my grandma passed away in April, five months after Brian died. I went back to Iowa to help Mom sort through Grandma's things and sell the farm. While I was there, I received a phone call. Brian's younger brother, Kenny, had died."

"Your brother-in-law?"

"Yes, Brian's death was more than he could bear. Grief-stricken, Kenny shot himself."

"Oh, Loretta—"

She watched as the blades of the ceiling fan rhythmically churned the stifling air. "When I heard that Kenny had taken his own life, I felt like somebody had kicked me in the gut. His death—his whole life—was sad. When he was nine, he'd been hit by a car and suffered brain damage which affected his motor skills. Because of that, Kenny slurred his words and walked with a limp. He was a bit of a social outcast. Kenny graduated from college, but nothing had come easy. With Brian gone, he must have felt hopeless and alone."

"How horrible for his parents . . . to lose both sons within six months of each other?"

Loretta nodded. "I wasn't any help to my in-laws. My fragile mom had suffered a mini stroke the night of Brian's funeral. Her health worsened until she passed away November 13 . . . one year and a day after Brian's death."

"I can't imagine so much grief within a twelve-month span."

"The year following Brian's death felt like a never-ending nightmare." She inhaled deeply and swallowed hard. "I could barely function. The busyness of life distracted me during the day, but I hated the night. I'd toss and turn in bed. Dark thoughts and death consumed my mind. When morning came, I had no energy or desire to get out of bed. I'd stick my leg out of the covers and say,

'Father, I can't. Help me!' That's when I learned that when I can't, he can. God's strength is perfected in weakness. God enabled me to get out of bed and get on with my day."

Loretta amazed me. How did she come away from this hellish year with such a teachable heart instead of embitterment?

Her eyes widened slightly as she shifted into teaching mode. She held up two fingers. "That's when I remembered two things I'd learned in my twenties. They helped me cope with grief and became the framework for my life."

"Two things? Wait a second." I grabbed my purse and groped in the dark hole for a pen and scratch paper. I settled on a smudged business envelope from our cable company. "Go ahead."

"The first thing, and perhaps most important, was remembering God's purpose for my life."

"And that purpose was . . . ?"

"Something I learned from Dr. Marchant King, my Bible professor. He had Lou Gehrig's disease and sat in a wheelchair. I can still see him in class, raising his crippled arm into the air and letting it fall to the desk as he declared in a booming voice, 'God's ultimate purpose for mankind is to be conformed into the image of his Son and to bring him praise.'"

"Can you repeat that?" I asked.

"Bottom line: God's goal is to make us like Jesus and to bring him praise." She watched me scribble on the envelope before adding, "I also wrote down what Dr. King said, but at the time, it was only head knowledge. I didn't grasp the meaning of those words until Brian died, twelve years later."

I set my pen down. Time to listen. I didn't want to wait twelve years—or endure some crisis—to understand the ultimate purpose of life.

"Three months after Brian's death, I was driving alone in our old Ford 500 truck when it struck me. Brian is *never* coming back.

I missed him so much that my heart physically ached. And the responsibility of being a working, single mom? I felt paralyzed, like I couldn't do it anymore. I pulled over to the side of the road and, shaking, I cried out to God, 'What do you want from me?'

"Immediately the Holy Spirit took me back to Dr. King's comment about God's ultimate purpose. And, just like that," Loretta snapped her fingers, "what I'd previously known only in my mind became the cry of my heart! I literally begged God, 'Yes, yes, do whatever it takes for me to be changed into the likeness of Jesus and for me to continually bring you praise." Loretta sighed like a load had been removed from her shoulders.

A knot formed in my throat. I wanted to stand up and applaud Loretta's faith. To write her name in Hebrews 11 alongside the other people in the Bible who'd lived by faith when they endured hardships. No question, I wanted Loretta's deep faith. But I didn't want to be *her*, not if it meant I'd have to suffer as much as she had.

God's voice caught me off guard. **Karen, I don't want you to be like Loretta. I want you to be you. And to make *you* like Jesus.**

Goosebumps gathered on my skin. Time stopped. The Almighty God of the universe had just spoken to my heart. I should have bowed low and humbly said, "Yes Lord, do with me as you will." Instead, my emotions recoiled. Fear and Trust engaged in a fierce game of tug-of-war.

I want to be like Jesus, but I don't want to suffer like he did, The Fearful Me tugged.

The Trusting Me countered, *Why should God spare me from pain if good comes from it?*

The Fearful Me yanked back, *But I can learn obedience by meditating on God's Word. I can become like Jesus that way, instead of through suffering.*

The Trusting Me jerked the rope with such force that my hands burned. *Why are you so afraid of what God wants to teach you?*

Unaware of my mental gymnastics, Loretta continued the thread of her own thoughts. "The second thing I learned that helped me through that horrific year has to do with Job's intolerable compliment."

I rubbed my temples to stop the battle in my mind. I picked up my pen, and wrote the words 'Job's intolerable compliment' on my envelope, but the words made no sense.

"Interesting term, but what does it mean?" I asked.

"The word intolerable refers to Job's unjust losses. He lost everything he valued. His children. His servants. His livestock. His fertile land. And, his health—he suffered from boils and physical pain." Loretta raked her hands through her hair. "Satan took all those things from Job and left him with nothing, all in an attempt to test whether or not he would trust God."

"I get the intolerable part." I groaned. "What's the compliment?"

"The compliment—intended for Job—came from God when he told Satan, 'Have you considered my servant, Job?' It's almost like God is bragging about Job . . . that his unwavering faith in God's goodness and sovereignty, his obedience, and his desire to praise God in every circumstance, was unequal to anyone else in the world."

I took a drink of lemonade. I'd never considered it a compliment to trust someone with hard things, but it was true. God knew Job would trust him. Job's steadfast trust delighted the heart of God.

Loretta patted her chest and whispered in a broken voice. "I wouldn't compare myself to Job, but the thought that such a Big God would trust me with hard things . . . like losing my husband, mother, grandma, and brother-in-law within a year's time . . . is huge to me."

I squirmed in my chair and looked at Murph, sound asleep by the couch.

Could God trust me to trust him during adversity? I hoped so. I remembered the time Dan had been deployed with the military during Desert Storm. I'd trusted God with his life. I also thought of those agonizing two weeks in NICU when our newborn's life was in doubt. I'd trusted God then. But what if Dan or Jason had died? Would I have continued to trust God? I didn't want to think about it.

Loretta interrupted my musings. "I want God to teach me and change me. I can't change myself. But I get to *choose*, like Job, how to respond to my circumstances. I can either bend and let God work in my life and change me. Or I can resist and lose out on his lessons." She paused. "Have you read Elizabeth Elliot's book, *Through Gates of Splendor?*"

"Yes, her husband, Jim, was killed along with four other missionaries by the Auca Indians in South America."

"Well, I met Elizabeth. We talked about the dark years in our lives. And we agreed that God prepared our hearts prior to our husbands' deaths by teaching us how to trust him in the smaller areas of our lives—before a huge trust was needed."

My heart thumped. *Why this conversation? Why now? Are you preparing me, God, for the next hardship? Are you going to take four of my loved ones in the same year? Will you allow Satan to test my allegiance like he did with Job?*

Imaginary what ifs rose to the surface like sharks circling for blood. My heart begged, *Don't touch my family!* Just telling God (and Satan) to leave my family alone made me skittish. I felt like I'd drawn a bull's eye on my loved ones' backs. *Oh, Lord, I'm not Job—or Loretta. I don't know if you can trust me with harder things than I've already faced.*

I stood up with tear-filled eyes and an empty glass, suddenly weary of the topic of suffering. "I'm not you, Loretta. Your faith is stronger than mine. And I don't want to endure—or earn—some intolerable compliment."

I escaped to the kitchen, turned on the faucet, and let the cool water flow over my wrists. It was that time of the month and I had whacked-out hormones. Actually it had been that painful time of the month for two weeks. It didn't take much to make me cry. Some days, I wanted to yell. Mostly, I stuffed my feelings and held on for dear life while my body plunged into new territory. Menopause—the word alone made me feel ancient. I wasn't ready to exchange my estrogen for a semi-empty nest. But what could I do?

My body was changing. My life, too. My two oldest kids would leave home the next month. Jonathan planned to transfer to another university. Jenny wanted to spend two years at a Christian ministry before attending college. I was excited for them, but each passing day felt like a count-down to that insufferable day when my heart-strings would be yanked out of my chest. But why be afraid or distressed? Loretta had shared two lessons that helped her handle adversity. Hopefully, those lessons would help me—not if, but when I needed them.

I returned to the living room with my empty picnic basket, embarrassed by my earlier outburst. But when Loretta spoke, her voice sounded warm and soft as butter sitting at room temperature. "Karen, you said my faith is stronger. Not true. I'm just older and farther down the road. Remember what Phyllis said, 'Life with God is a process.' The secret is knowing God's purpose for our lives and relying on the Holy Spirit's power to trust him."

Sleepy-eyed Murph sat up and licked Loretta's hand which dangled off the edge of the couch. Her hand twitched and she looked down at him. "Murph, you're such a love. I forgot you were there."

My spirit relaxed. Watching the two of them, I knew that everything I'd ever learned from Loretta boiled down to this— resting at the Master's feet. She'd run to the Lord over and over again until she'd been conditioned to stay close to him.

I gathered my things. "Time for me to leave and let you rest."

"Consider yourself hugged," she responded from her couch perch, and we promised to connect soon.

As I climbed into my car to leave, I smiled. I'd come to Loretta's house with the intent of blessing her, but once again she'd blessed me. Despite Loretta's weakness, God had used her to strengthen my faith.

I turned the key in the ignition. As I did, the Holy Spirit ignited my heart. *God, make me more like Jesus,* I prayed. *Whatever it takes.* I pushed down the accelerator and the van lurched forward. *Whatever it takes.*

Take Away Nuggets

 Every circumstance is an opportunity to become like Jesus.

 "For God knew his people in advance, and he chose them to become like his Son" (Romans 8:29).

Food for Thought

1. Loretta expected God to teach and change her through painful circumstances. Think of a time when you suffered. Was your heart teachable, or did you resist the hand of God shaping you? What are you doing today to ensure that your heart is teachable in the future?

2. Read Romans 8:28–29 and Ephesians 1:5–12. How do these verses support Dr. King's statement that God's ultimate purpose for mankind is to conform us into Christ's image and to bring him praise?

3. Loretta talked about Job's intolerable compliment. Explain why God would praise Job for trusting him through adversity. Think of an incident when you trusted God with a hard thing. How does it make you feel to know that God knew you'd trust him with that difficult circumstance? Read the first chapter of Job. Consider how God planned, purposed, and worked all things for Job's good.

CHAPTER 8

The Battle of Spiritual Indifference

The great thing to remember is that, though our feelings come and go, His love for us does not. It is not wearied by our sins, or our indifference; and therefore, it is quite relentless in its determination that we shall be cured of those sins, at whatever cost to us, at whatever cost to Him.
—C. S. Lewis

My head throbbed as the windshield wipers swished back and forth. *Why did I agree to have lunch with Loretta?* I didn't feel like talking to anyone, especially if we had to talk about God.

Oops! Red flag! How did I go from being a woman on fire for God who loved talking about him to being bored with spiritual things? I definitely needed to see my spiritual mentor.

I turned on the defroster. Between the winter holidays and our action-packed calendars, months had flown by since I'd seen Loretta. Emails volleyed back and forth before we finally found a mutually free date in late January. How could I back out now? I ignored my compulsion to turn around. Why did I feel this way?

For the past month, I'd been self-absorbed and withdrawn from family and friends. I'd skipped women's Bible study the previous week and lied about being sick so I didn't have to volunteer in Jason's classroom. I'd retreated from God and the world, buried my nose in a historical novel, and watched old classic movies while I gorged on buttered popcorn. I told myself it wasn't my fault. The ceaseless rain depressed me. And, I needed a purpose that didn't involve oven mitts and a grocery list.

Besides, it's not like my family noticed my absence. As long as I served a hot dinner and kept up with the laundry, no one complained. They recognized my "Gollum" mood and avoided me. I assumed God felt the same way towards me because for the past two weeks he seemed distant . . . as though biding his time until I got over it. Whatever *it* was.

I shook my head like it was an Etch A Sketch drawing toy, but I couldn't erase the pessimistic thoughts on my mind. My stomach grumbled. I'd slept in and had to skip breakfast in order to meet Loretta on time. The woman was never late.

I drove into the parking lot of the casual Greek restaurant we'd agreed upon and spotted Loretta seated in her Honda Accord. I parked and turned the engine off. Then I used my purse as an improvised umbrella and held it above my head while I hopped over several puddles on the way to her car. I pasted a smile on my face, knocked on Loretta's passenger window, and waited for her to unlock it so I could slip inside.

"Great day to be a duck," she said with less enthusiasm than normal. She reached over to hug me. "The restaurant isn't open for another fifteen minutes."

I bit my tongue. *Glad I rushed to get here.*

While the rain hammered her car's roof, Loretta discussed her nagging cough which made it difficult to sleep at night. She rarely talked about her health. But today, she complained of dizziness and the challenge of finding the right thyroid medication. I half-listened, nodded, and watched the giant raindrops smash against the windshield. I couldn't wait to return home and crawl back in bed.

When the restaurant opened, we hurried inside and ordered our food at the counter. Then we saddled up to a high-top table next to the picture window and waited for our meals. The dark shadows beneath Loretta's eyes confirmed her lack of sleep. If I'd been more sensitive, I would have encouraged my friend to continue talking about her health. Or, switched to a more lighthearted subject. But I chose instead to talk about me.

"I don't know if it's hormones or winter blues," I whined, "but I've been depressed for over a month. I feel unappreciated by my family. My birthday is next month, but do you think there will be a celebration unless I plan it? Noooo! I'm tired of giving. Tired of serving the church and school." I closed my eyes to squeeze back the tears. "I'm just tired and—"

"Empty?" She interjected.

I opened my eyes and nodded. If we'd been alone, I would have burst into tears.

"Been there," Loretta said with compassion in her weary eyes. And if those two words were the only words she'd said that day, it would have been enough. I needed to know I wasn't alone or crazy. Someone actually heard me and understood!

But her next words gave me heartburn as if I'd swallowed a jalapeño.

"Are you meeting with God each day?"

Each day? I crossed my arms. *I thought you said you'd been there?* I didn't have the energy to floss or engage my husband in conversation. How was I supposed to muster the energy to meet with God?

Before I could respond, a bubbly twenty-something server with a Hollywood-perfect smile and a dyed pink streak in her blond hair brought our food. Loretta perked up and asked about her day. Their cheery banter grated on my taunt nerves. I wanted to put on my sunglasses and move to another table where I could enjoy being by myself.

When our server left, Loretta clutched my right hand and prayed over our meal. I closed my eyes, but the tangy steam from my bowl of lemon chicken soup distracted me. I peaked at my plate of chicken kabobs and wished I'd ordered grilled veggies as a side dish instead of rice pilaf. My mouth watered and I licked my lips right when Loretta ended her prayer with, "Thank you, Father."

"Thank you," I mindlessly repeated and traded her hand for my soup spoon. "Soup's getting cold," I added.

Loretta slowly stirred her soup and watched me eat. "I hate to see you so despondent, but you know, only God satisfies our hearts. Regardless of our situation, there's no place and no one who can satisfy like the Father. Remember, to the degree we seek God, he'll meet us."

I nodded and continued to slurp my soup. Familiar words. How could I forget? We'd often discussed the importance of seeking God and practicing his presence. And on most days, Loretta's gentle reminder would have been like adding yeast to dough—my soft pliable heart would have doubled in size. However, on this gray day, I rejected her words like a plate of cold leftovers. Come to think of it, my soup tasted bland too. I tossed my spoon in the half-empty bowl and pushed it aside.

Loretta arched a brow at my stony expression. "I've never seen you this resistant when we've talked about seeking God." When I didn't respond, she laid her spoon down and her expression turned to one of pain and concern. "You might have winter blues, but I think your real problem is indifference towards the Lord."

Ouch!

Talk about a left hook. I didn't see that coming. I took my fork and scraped the chunks of grilled chicken off my two wooden skewers. *Who does she think she is?* Then again, I'd given Loretta permission to be honest with me from the beginning.

"I'm on your side," she said. "You know that, right?"

Loretta's empathy failed to soothe my ruffled feathers. My mood was stormier than when I'd arrived. I stared at my plate like a sullen child while I ate. I wouldn't have faulted God if he'd sent a lightning bolt through the window to zap me. In fact, I'm surprised Loretta didn't ask for a doggy bag so she could take her food home instead of hanging out with me.

Loretta's voice rose a notch. "Like you, I've also experienced spiritual indifference. But when that happens, I remind myself that God longs for our fellowship. It's our privilege to spend time with him. Christ paid for that privilege with his blood. I'd no sooner give up my alone time with God than brushing my teeth. But I have to be intentional. You know what I mean?"

Our eyes met and I didn't look away from Loretta's beseeching brown eyes. My words came out more forcefully than I intended. "You don't understand. I pray, but God is silent. I try to read my Bible, but it's become a chore. I dread going to church and I hurry out before I have to face people. Who knows which came first—my indifference or the melancholy? But I'm stuck somewhere between *who cares* and *ho-hum bored.*"

Loretta took a deep breath and rolled up the sleeves of her red sweatshirt as though she was entering battle. I assumed she fought for me rather than against me.

"I get it," she said. "But our Christian walk isn't a straight line. We shouldn't be surprised when there are high and lows, and spiritual dry spells." Loretta turned and coughed into her paper napkin. Then she took a long drink of water.

I stared at the heavy downpour outside the picture window. *Yeah, maybe I'm going through a spiritual dry spell. I just have to wait it out.*

"You know, Karen, there are many things that can affect our desire to spend time with God." She gestured toward the window. "The weather, our health, our sin, our circumstances . . . they all play a role in our spiritual vitality. And Satan will use whatever it takes to derail us so we stop seeking God."

I rubbed the knot in my neck. The grey skies and long winter nights definitely contributed to my glum mood. My journal showed I often felt depressed in January. But no matter how contradictory, I didn't want the weather and the seasons to dictate my joy.

Loretta cleared her throat and continued, "I also think spiritual indifference happens . . . at least for me . . . when God's character and his grace becomes too familiar. I start to take him for granted. Other times, I become indifferent because I'm too wrapped up in myself. My needs. My agenda. I'm in a hurry to get on with my day so I don't put in the effort to seek God with my whole heart."

I appreciated Loretta's honesty. However, I didn't care if she'd wrestled with spiritual indifference. I preferred to change the subject. I was about to ask Loretta if she'd read any good books lately when she dipped pita bread into her tzatziki sauce and said, "Sometimes, meeting with God feels like work. Other days, I'm running to him like a carefree child. I can't wait to be with him."

Loretta paused to chew her pita bread and watched me sprinkle pepper over my Greek side salad. I set the pepper shaker down and pressed the back of my hand against my itchy nostrils. "Sorry," I said, sniffing. "I thought I was going to sneeze. Go on."

Loretta sighed. "We've talked about the difference between reading daily devotions and meeting with God. One is head knowledge, the other is a heart connection. Intimacy with God happens when we make time to be still before him and allow our emotions and thoughts to be engaged. Whenever it's difficult to be in the moment, I find it helps to remember God's promises and the good things he's done in my life. Remembering his blessings makes me grateful and able to rejoice."

I couldn't argue with that truth. Who cared how I described my lackluster heart—spiritually dry, indifferent, bored? I knew I needed to seek God with my whole heart, mind, and soul if I wanted to experience his peace and joy. Besides, God deserved my praise regardless of my circumstances and emotions. I should have stopped right then and asked Loretta to pray for me. Instead, I pulled my phone from my purse to check the time and responded to someone's text.

I set the phone on the table. "Yes, I know. We've talked about the importance of meeting with God. So how should I handle my lack of desire to meet with him?"

Loretta remained quiet for a few minutes. Then she pushed her plate aside and leaned forward on the table with her hands clasped. "Whenever I wrestle with spiritual indifference, I do three things. First, I read a different translation of the Bible, particularly the ones where I haven't already highlighted passages. That way, I read God's Word with fresh eyes instead of falling back on my preconceived ideas."

"Good idea," I said. "I'm getting more iced tea. Do you need anything?"

Loretta shook her head. As I walked to the soda fountain, I felt pretty sure she was watching me. Reading different Bible translations sounded wise. Then again, I didn't see how reading the New Living Translation Bible instead of my New American Standard would rescue me from this funk. I tossed a slice of lemon into my tea and told myself to be nice. Loretta didn't deserve my sour disposition.

When I returned to the table, Loretta picked up where she'd left off. "The second thing that helps me has to do with brokenness.

I told you about my friend, Phyllis, right? She's with the Lord now, but Phyllis once told me that she stayed in God's Word until he broke her. Well, Phyllis had such a huge heart for God that I remember thinking . . . if she needed to be broken and it was that important to her, then I wanted that too—especially when I felt nonchalant toward God."

I broke my pita bread in half and dipped it into the tzatziki sauce. "When you say, 'broken' what do you mean?"

"Well, my heart breaks when I think about the cross—how Christ suffered. How he loved me so much that he died for me." Loretta's voice caught in her throat. "That thought moves me to tears every time."

She removed her glasses and wiped her tired eyes. Why did this strong woman always seem so tender and cry so easily whenever we talked about her Lord? Why did my heart feel like granite?

"When I have trouble drawing near to God," she said, "I bow down and cry, 'I can't even do this Father.' That's when he comes and shows me who I am . . . his adopted daughter . . . and draws me ever so sweetly."

The bubbly blond waitress came to our table and removed our dishes. She seemed more reserved. Were we talking too loudly? I glanced around the room at the other diners and cringed. Hopefully, if they were listening, they only heard Loretta's words. Not mine.

A gust of wind rattled the cloth awning over the restaurants's side entrance. I turned toward the picture window next to us in time to watch a black metal patio chair flip over in the courtyard. A large decorative rock had been placed near a crepe myrtle that grew from a square patch of soil in the midst of the concrete patio. Raindrops blasted the crusty rock and rolled down its rough sides into the soil where I imagined the tree roots guzzled the life-giving water. By spring, the tree should grow and blossom. The rock would still be hard. Which one was I choosing to be? A blossoming tree full of life or an immovable granite stone?

I rubbed my stiff neck. "You mentioned there were three things that helped you," I said to prove that I'd been paying attention. "You read different Bible translations and pray for brokenness. What's the third thing?"

"Worship." Loretta held up three fingers resembling the letter W. "Don't underestimate the value of worship before you open the Bible. Singing hymns or praise music softens our hearts to meet with God. Psalm 13:6 says, 'I will sing to the Lord, because he has dealt bountifully with me.' So I sing to the Father. And whenever my cough keeps me from singing, I read the lyrics of a worship song out loud to him. Either way, songs are like the kindling that starts the fire of passion for God within me."

I nodded. Surely one of her suggestions would tenderize my heart, but one objection hounded me and it poured out of my mouth. "Good words, Loretta, but have you ever done those three things. . . and been frustrated because God remains silent?"

Loretta wrapped her fingers around her water glass. "I went through a dark period for about six weeks last summer when God appeared silent . . . and in the wings, so to speak. I knew to trust God's presence and wait for his fellowship, but a lack of intimacy does take its toll. Plus, I missed God's fellowship because I've tasted it so often. I think we humans—" Loretta stifled a cough and drank the rest of her water. When she set her glass down, she groaned. "Shoot bother, I just lost that thought."

"No worries," I said. "I know you're tired. We should go."

Loretta smiled weakly and pulled her car keys out of her purse when she suddenly stopped and jiggled her keys. "I just remembered what I wanted to say."

I raised my brows.

"I shared three things to rekindle our desire for God. But when God seems silent, I think it boils down to this—humans want to *experience* God's presence. God wants us to *believe* he is present."

My pulse quickened. For the first time that day, I felt a spark of energy. I knew she was right. Faith is how we please God. And deep down more than anything I did want to please him.

We headed out the door and stood beneath the awning. The rain had stopped, leaving a fresh, musky scent. "Thanks for being my God-friend, Loretta. You always point me to the Lord."

"I love being with you," she responded. "I hope you know that."

"Even when I'm a brat?"

She laughed and engulfed me in a hug. "I'll be praying for you," she whispered. "Promise me you'll seek God regardless of how you feel. Just say, 'I love you' to him, and sing his praises."

"I promise, Loretta." I put my hand across my heart like a sacred vow. "I promise."

The next morning brought more thunderstorms. Bound by my promise, more than by sincere emotion, I asked God to forgive my indifference. Then I grabbed my English Standard Version Bible that hadn't been marked up and read Psalm 51:10-12 out loud. "Create in me a clean heart, Oh God, and renew a right spirit within me. Cast me not away from your presence, and take not your Holy Spirit from me. Restore to me the joy of your salvation, and uphold me with a willing spirit."

I sang "How Great is Our God" by Chris Tomlin. When I finished singing, I waited. I listened, fully expecting God to miraculously crack my granite wall and fill me with giddiness. Or, at the very least, whisper something pleasant to my heart.

I felt nothing.

Where are you Lord? Do You hear my cry?

The following morning, I had to choose again to honor my promise to Loretta to seek God. No doubt Loretta was praying for me at that exact moment because suddenly a verse popped into my head: "Taste and see that the Lord is good." Before I could see God's goodness, I had to make a conscious effort to taste. "Lord, wake up my taste buds," I prayed and opened my ESV Bible to Psalm 63:1. "Oh God, you are my God; earnestly I seek you; my soul thirsts for you; my flesh faints for you, as in a dry and weary land where there is no water."

I went to the window and looked at the saturated ground. *What a stark contrast to my dry, thirsty soul.* I opened my palms and raised my hands. "Lord, rain down on me. Pour your living water into me. Fill me to overflowing with your Spirit."

My desperate prayer triggered nothing inside of me. I still felt dead inside.

I knew the reality of God's presence didn't depend on me having a touchy-feely experience. But I desperately needed some hint of his nearness to keep me going. I leaned my forehead against the cool window and watched a solitary raindrop trickle like a tear down the glass pane. Loretta had waited six weeks for her dark season to pass. How long would I have to wait?

Oak trees stretched bare limbs toward ominous clouds that draped the wet foothills like a burial shroud. I couldn't see the sun or feel its warmth, but that didn't mean it wasn't shining. "Lord, I *know* you're here even though I can't see your face. And even though I can't feel your presence—I will trust your heart knowing this dark season shall pass."

Take Away Nuggets

 When you can't see God's face, you need to trust his heart.

 "The Lord is close to the brokenhearted; he rescues those whose spirits are crushed" (Psalm 34:18).

Food for Thought

1. Circle the number that describes the condition of your heart right now, with one being "indifferent toward God" and ten being "very tender toward God."

   1 2 3 4 5 6 7 8 9 10

2. Describe a time when you've felt spiritually dry. What helped you reconnect with God? Why is it important to trust God's heart when we can't see his face? Hebrews 13:5 says, "For he has said, 'I will never leave you nor forsake you.'" What are some other promises you can rely on when you're spiritually depressed or God seems distant?

3. Like Karen, Loretta said she also experienced spiritual indifference. She suggested three ways that helped overcome spiritual indifference. What were they? Why do you think obedience should take priority over emotions when it comes to worshipping God?

4. Although our tendency is to hide when we feel depressed or angry, what's the value of inviting someone safe to hear our hurts and to speak into our life? Are you a safe place (free from judgment or gossip) for others to share their hurts?

CHAPTER 9

Adding Sweetener to the Marriage Pie

Let the wife make the husband glad to come home,
and let him make her sorry to see him leave.
—Martin Luther

I arrived at the restaurant fifteen minutes early for my lunch date with Loretta, but only because traffic had been less congested than I'd expected. *Sweet!* I craved a brief respite especially after a stressful morning. I reclined the car seat, took a deep breath, and exhaled.

Chirp! A text from Dan: "Need milk."

Need milk? Grrrr. Now, in addition to my stop at Ace to return a sprinkler head, picking up Dan's shirts from the dry cleaner, and returning overdue library books, I'd have to swing by the grocery store. Plus, I needed to phone the high school and let them know I'd substitute teach on Friday.

I jerked my car seat into an upright position. *A please and thank you might be nice.* I drummed my fingers on the steering wheel and stared out the window at the buds on the crepe myrtle in front of me.

Well, at least he's speaking to me. When I'd asked Dan a question earlier about our dental insurance, he'd snapped, "Look it up." Then he complained that our income taxes were due soon and he needed to work on them. "Unless *you* plan on filling out the tax forms this year."

"I'd love to," I said, echoing his sarcasm. "And you can help with the housework. When's the last time you held a toilet brush?"

His jaw tightened. "You want my job? Fighting rush hour traffic? Paying the bills? Funny how money pops out from the ATM when you need it."

"I may not get paid for taking care of the kids and this house, but I work hard. Your clean clothes don't appear in your dresser drawer by magic, you know."

We stormed off into our separate corners. Then, I grabbed the car keys, thankful I had a lunch date with Loretta so I could leave the house.

Did Mama ever feel unappreciated by Dad? Did Dad grumble about his job? I had no memory of them arguing when I was a kid, but I couldn't imagine a marriage without an occasional battle of the sexes. I closed my eyes and told myself to breathe. *I feel so tired.* And yet, when I'd woken at six a.m. that morning I'd found Dan already in front of the computer, moving funds around to pay for Jonathan's college expenses and Jason's braces. Jenny would need a car when she went off to college. Not to mention the monthly household expenses. I'd tip toed around Dan, careful not to bother him in his work mode. Looking back, I could have been more supportive, but he'd been so irritable with me that I felt like I could do nothing right.

Tap, tap, tap!

The knocking on the driver's window made me flinch. I opened the door.

"Sorry," Loretta said with a sheepish grin. "Didn't mean to startle you."

I tossed the cell phone into my purse and breathed in the smoky, wood-burning scent wafting from the restaurant. *That's what I need. Comfort food to soothe my taunt nerves.*

We went inside and settled into a booth next to a large-paned window with wooden venetian blinds. "So many choices," said Loretta as she flipped through her spiral menu. "What are you having?"

I pointed to a picture on the menu and read the description. "An oven baked calzone stuffed with spicy pepperoni, melted mozzarella, mushrooms, and rich tomato sauce."

She licked her lips. "Sounds larapin."

Loretta's silly word for scrumptious normally made me smile but my earlier run-in with Dan had stripped me of my sense of humor. When our meal arrived, I barely tasted the calzone because I rambled throughout the meal like two beaters in a mixing bowl, whipping myself into a frenzy the more I complained about Dan.

"You know, my husband's employer declared bankruptcy. Dan took a huge pay cut and the company's stocks fell in value. It's worrisome not knowing if Dan will have a job with them a year from now, but our reduced income and the scary unknown doesn't stress me out as much as Dan's pessimistic attitude. Sometimes, he acts like I'm the enemy. When I tell Dan to be grateful and try not to worry, he fusses, 'easy for you to say.'"

Loretta had finished eating her lemon-pepper steak with mashed potatoes. She set her knife and fork on the plate and leaned back in the red leather booth. "I haven't met your husband, but I know men are made from a different fabric than women. Much of a man's identity is wrapped up in his role as breadwinner. A good man provides and protects his family. So any failure or injustice in his job is bound to be extremely stressful."

Noting her sympathetic tone towards Dan, I defended myself. "Well, I try to support Dan by staying within our budget. I've also tried to supplement our income through substitute teaching. Only, it doesn't pay well. And when I've offered to get a full-time job, he says it's not necessary at this point." I used my breadstick to mop the leftover tomato sauce on my plate and laid the soggy breadstick down. "I know being the main breadwinner for a family of five is a heavy backpack. I get it. And he probably feels alone knowing it's all on him. But I get tired of being the cheerleader especially when nothing I say or do cheers him up."

Loretta clasped her hands on the table and leaned towards me, her voice tender and kind. "Karen, what do you love about your husband?"

My eyes widened in surprise. I expected sage advice on how to live with Grumpy. Not this out-of-the-blue question about my husband's finer qualities.

"Well, . . . he's a Christian. I can't imagine being married to someone who didn't share the same faith."

Loretta nodded, encouraging me to continue.

"He's a great dad. He puts the needs of our kids above his own." Another nod.

"And he's good at handling our finances which is why I'm not overly concerned about our income." I paused, expecting Loretta to break in with a comment, but she just raised her eyebrows and waited for me to continue.

I cleared my throat. "He has a great mind. I'm amazed at how knowledgeable he is on so many subjects. And if something needs fixing around the house, he figures it out. I always hear about husbands who procrastinate, but not Dan. He'll change a lightbulb before I realize it's burnt out."

"Those things are all good," Loretta said. "But what do you like about him *as your husband* . . . and *close companion?*"

"You mean other than his sexy blue eyes and the fact that he puts up with me?" I laughed and looked down at my wedding ring. The diamond on the gold band reflected the light from the stained-glass pendant over our table. "Well, I enjoy Dan's company. We never run out of things to talk about. Sometimes, I think he knows me better than I know myself."

I took a drink of iced tea and smiled. "He makes me laugh. One time we'd been talking about our dental hygienist because she wears so much protective head gear while she cleans our teeth. She looks like a mad scientist suited up to work with infectious diseases. We wondered if she was protecting us from her germs or protecting herself from our germs. So on his next appointment, Dan walked into the dentist office wearing yard gloves, ski goggles, and a paint mask over his mouth and nose. He had the office staff in stitches."

Loretta laughed with me. "He sounds wonderful."

"Yes, I'm very blessed," I said, regretting my earlier outburst.

"Cherish those thoughts. And from now on, I want you to consider praying for your husband without defining his needs."

I wrinkled my forehead. "What do you mean, 'without defining his needs?'"

"Well, think about the times we've prayed together and how I pray for you. My prayers aren't focused on specifics—like whether you should teach high school drama next year. Instead, I ask God to give you wisdom as you make decisions."

"Are you saying that it's wrong to pray for specifics?" I asked.

"Not at all," Loretta replied. "But when we *only* pray about specific things for our husbands . . . like finding a job that pays more or having him get involved in a men's group at church . . . we're pursuing our own agenda instead of having God's interest at heart—the development of his character."

I couldn't argue with that. I wanted God to develop Dan's character, but in all honesty, my prayers often included some pretty specific direction about how God should do that.

"Remember," Loretta continued. "God made you and Dan distinctly different from each other. You're different just by being male and female. You have different personalities. You respond to life differently. You worship God in different ways. Don't try to change your husband." Loretta smiled and tapped her finger on the table. "Karen, God is working in your husband . . . the same way God is working in your children's hearts. Your task is to love and pray for him."

"But specifics *are* important," I countered. "I've prayed that Dan would have an opportunity to share the gospel with a certain co-worker. I've asked God to help Dan pass his annual check rides at work."

"That's a given," Loretta said, pulling a loose thread from her blue jean jacket. "But try not to ask God to change your husband or his circumstances according to your timetable and what you assume he needs. God's purposes are so much bigger than anything we can imagine. So pray that God will speak to Dan's heart and use this bankruptcy to develop qualities such as self-control, patience, kindness. Then, get out of the way."

Trusting God to work in my husband's heart sounded simplistic. Then again, perhaps the problem stemmed from me. My need to be in control and certain of the outcome. Because to let go would require more faith than a hands-on approach.

I glanced at the booth caddy-cornered from us. A man advanced in years, facing my direction, wore a Vietnam Vet baseball cap. I watched the tremor of his gnarled hand as he lifted his coffee mug to his lips. *A widower? Divorced?* Why did I assume he was either just because he ate alone? Odd that my heart went out to this complete stranger while my husband was home alone, doing our taxes. I doubt Dan would even think to stop for lunch. A wave of conviction and sadness that I'd grumbled about my wonderful man washed over me.

"So, Loretta, you're saying that I should claim God's promises and pray scripture over Dan instead of asking for specific things *I think* he needs?"

"Yes, because when you pray without defining your husband's needs you tell God, 'I trust you to work in my husband's life. Do whatever's necessary, according to your will, in order for him to be made into your likeness.' Because if that's God's eternal purpose, then that's how we want God to move." Smiling, she leaned back and casually crossed her arms. "At least that's how I see it."

"Okay," I said, waving my white cloth napkin in mock surrender. "I'll pray for my husband instead of trying to fix him. Or, telling God how to make Dan my idea of the perfect spouse."

Loretta didn't smile at my antics. Instead she uncrossed her arms and looked at me in way that assured me this prayer wasn't a joke. "Karen, I realize this kind of prayer might be different from what you're used to, but this is what God taught me when Brian suffered with depression."

"Brian? Depressed?" Until now, I'd only heard about Brian's strong faith and spiritual leadership. This was a side of him I didn't know. And yet? I rubbed my brow to rouse a distant conversation. "Oh yeah, you once mentioned Brian's depression, but you didn't go into any detail."

"Well, it's a long story, but I can give you the condensed version."

I smiled. "You can even give me the lonnnng version if you'd like." Loretta's stories always inspired me. And frankly, I needed a healthy dose of inspiration in the wife/husband arena.

"When Brian finished seminary, he wanted to be a jungle pilot under Mission Aviation Fellowship. But first, he had to attend the Moody Aviation School in Chicago to earn his pilot license. When we prayed together, Brian told God that he had no particular need to be a missionary pilot. He only wanted what God wanted. If Moody accepted him, Brian said he'd take that as God's will. He also promised to do his part and finish strong. So began an entire year filled with tests, screening, and waiting. In the summer of 1967, we got the green light."

"Did you go with him to Chicago?"

She shook her head. "No, it was financially impractical to live near Brian, or for me to stay in California. So we packed up our household goods. He went to Chicago and I took the kids to Des Moines where my parents lived." Loretta frowned. "It wasn't the best idea."

"Why not?" I asked.

"Living apart made it harder for Brian and me to support each other. I missed him and felt overwhelmed living in my parents' basement with three fussy children under the age of four. Plus Brian discovered the course was more challenging than he'd anticipated and that he wasn't meeting his own expectations. One weekend, Brian came to Des Moines to discuss whether he should continue the program. Instead of living up to our commitment to God, we weighed the pros and cons from a human perspective and decided to return to California. Sadly, that decision turned into one of our worst years together."

A middle-aged waitress with a tired smile came to the table with a water pitcher. Loretta nodded and held out her empty glass. "No thanks," I said when the waitress looked at me. When she left, I prompted Loretta. "You were saying."

"During seminary, Brian had worked as a truck driver for an oil refinery. Before he left for Chicago, he'd asked his boss to hold his job in case things didn't work out. Later, Brian admitted that was a mistake. Knowing he could return to his previous job gave him an 'easy out.'"

I nodded. Sometimes we all want to take the easy way out. "On the trip back to California, Brian drove alone and mulled over everything that had happened. I think Brian felt he'd done his part. God had not. By the time we reached California, he blamed God rather than bearing the responsibility of our own decision to leave Moody Aviation. Over the next few weeks, I watched his anger morph into depression. Brian worked hard to provide for our family, but he withdrew from the kids and me. He slept a lot. And he told me one Sunday, 'I'm not going to church. I'm finished with spiritual games.' Nothing I did seemed to help."

It wasn't hard for me to imagine Loretta's anguish as she helplessly watched her husband slide into depression. I loved Dan, just as she loved Brian, but sometimes there's simply nothing a wife can do. We have to let our husbands work out for themselves whatever it is they need to do, and all we can do is come alongside them and pray.

Loretta continued. "As the months dragged by without any resolution I became increasingly frustrated. I also felt humiliated knowing there were people at church who judged Brian for not being there. My lowest point came one evening when I realized that Brian, the most important person in my life and my mentor, was incapable of being my spiritual leader."

Loretta closed her eyes for a moment before going on. "That night is imprinted on my heart. Brian and the kids were asleep. I was exhausted from all the emotional drama of that day. I sank into my child, Jeff's, wooden rocker and watched the sun set outside our living room window. As the room grew darker and darker, dread filled my gut when I realized there was no quick fix. In that dark place, I felt alone. Abandoned. Lost."

I tried to picture Loretta's five-foot-eleven body squeezed into a child's rocker. That image struck me. How fitting that this spiritually mature woman had to possess a child-like faith before she could trust God with her husband's health.

"That night I realized I was wrong to place so much confidence in Brian's spiritual leadership instead of in God himself." Loretta squinted, her face awash in sunlight. I found the cord to the window's venetian blinds and slanted the wooden slats.

"Thanks." She blinked. "Anyway, my only option was running to God and relying on him to satisfy my heart."

"Is that when you started to pray without defining your husband's needs?"

Loretta nodded. "God's Spirit impressed those words on my heart after a godly woman told me, 'God owns Brian. He'll restore him. Your job is to *pray* for him.' So I used my controlling personality to control my mouth and my emotions." Loretta gestured like she was zipping her lips. "Keeping my mouth shut was enormous because I'd often spouted untimely words which made the situation worse."

Our waitress hurried past our table with a platter filled with sizzling chicken fajitas, leaving a scented trail of sautéed green peppers and onions in her wake. I looked at Loretta and moaned. "Is your mouth watering too?"

She grinned. "I don't remember seeing fajitas on the menu."

"We could hang around for supper," I joked. "Anyway, you controlled your tongue and you prayed. Any other advice?"

Loretta smiled, but it was a sad, reflective smile as she wiped the table where her glass had left water rings. "The China Inland Faith Mission motto says: 'Move man through God by prayer alone.' I took those words to heart. The more time I spent praying for God to work in Brian's heart instead of trying to change him, the less demanding I became and the more peace I felt. Sometimes, I'd lay beside him in bed and just hold him. Brian knew that I was praying for him. He once told me that he'd seen a change in me. I think he meant a softening in my personality because I could be rather feisty."

I smiled at my feisty mentor who suddenly turned quite serious.

"Brian eventually returned to Moody Aviation and received his pilot's license. But Karen, praying for Brian changed *me*. And, God used those prayers to *prepare me* for the dark days ahead after Brian died. So pray consistently for your husband. It's that important."

I swallowed the lump in my throat and nodded. Who needed comfort food when I had Loretta to point me back to God's will—honoring my husband and praying for him. I couldn't wait to get home and give Dan some sugar. I also wanted to remind him that we were on the same team and that I had his back.

But first, I had to run those pesky errands. As I stood in line at the dry cleaner, I prayed for Dan to be aware of God's love for him. At Ace Hardware, I prayed God would continue to strengthen Dan's good character. But as I drove away from the library, Dan's jabbing comment, *"Unless you want to do the taxes,"* entered my mind and stayed there. By the time I stood in the grocery line with a gallon of milk, I'd lost my bridal glow and good intentions. Perhaps Loretta was praying for me at that moment because when I switched the plastic milk jug to my left hand, my wedding ring shifted, and so did my thoughts as I reflected on Loretta's question, "What do you love about your husband?"

My throat constricted. "Excuse me," I told the customer behind me as I left the line. "I forgot something."

A half hour later, I arrived home. My hard-working man sat at his desk, surrounded by paperwork on the floor. He glanced up at me from the computer and grunted. "Get my text?"

"I got milk, and . . . I bought you a treat." I placed a jar of his favorite dried peanuts on the desk.

"That was nice of you." Dan's voice softened, and he sounded surprised, but he kept his eyes on the computer screen as if I wasn't there.

I started to leave the room and give Dan his personal space when Loretta's words echoed in my mind, "Pray for your husband. It's that important."

I walked behind Dan's chair, placed my hands on his shoulders, and slowly massaged his tight muscles. As my fingers pressed in, I silently prayed: *Lord, help this man who works so hard for our family. Help Dan see the fruits of his labor, and in lean times, help him to remember that you are still in control. Help him find fulfillment in his work and in his identity in you.*

Dan sighed. I could almost feel each word of my prayer travel from my heart through my fingers and into his own soul.

The corners of my mouth turned up in a smile at the irony of the thought that skittered through my mind. *I've got your back, Dan. I've got your back. And praise the Lord—he's got your back too.*

Take Away Nuggets

 Pray for people's character growth instead of only specifics.

 "I urge you, first of all, to pray for all people. Ask God to help them; intercede on their behalf, and give thanks for them" (1 Timothy 2:1).

Food for Thought

1. Why did Loretta urge Karen to pray for Dan without defining his needs? Whether you are married or single, how does this advice monitor our motives when we pray for others?

2. Richard Foster says, "When we genuinely believe that inner transformation is God's work, and not ours, we can put to rest our passion to set others straight." How can this perspective help you in your marriage and other relationships?

3. Read John 17:6—26 and note how Jesus prayed for his disciples and other believers. What does he ask for on their behalf?

4. Read Philippians 4:8. Make a list of your husband's excellent qualities. Then plan a special dinner and give him the list to read.

CHAPTER 10

Shall We Dance?

Praise lies upon a higher plain than thanksgiving.
When I give thanks, my thoughts still circle around
myself to some extent. But in praise my soul ascends to
self-forgetting adoration, seeing and praising only the
majesty and power of God, His grace and redemption.
—Ole Hallesby

I spooned a mound of molten sweetness onto my tongue.
Icy vanilla merged with the hot fudge and slid down my
throat. "Mmm, this sundae's so good," I moaned. "We
should meet for dessert more often."

Loretta nodded. Her bright smile shone like the restaurant's
golden arches at night. "You won't hear any complaints from me."
She glanced over her shoulder at the fast food counter. "I also love
their fries. I'm tempted to get some before I leave."

"Go for it! Live life on the edge, you wild woman!" I teased.

Loretta threw her head back and laughed. "Maybe I will, but I have to finish this first." She swirled salty peanut chips into a pool of fudge. "How was your Labor Day weekend?"

"I'm glad you asked. It was great. No! It was better than great. My feet didn't touch the ground the entire weekend. Even now, I'm happier than a dog with two tails."

Loretta shifted her body in the hard-backed booth and grinned. "That explains the sparkle in your eyes."

I framed my face with my two hands, fluttering my eyelashes at her. "Are you referring to my effervescent joy?"

"You crack me up." She laughed. "What happened to bring about this radiant glow?"

"Well, I can guarantee you it's not because I'm pregnant!"

Loretta chuckled over my silliness. "Okay, my funny God friend! Tell me about your weekend."

I scraped the ribbon of fudge clinging to the inside of my cup and let my tongue caress the rich chocolate on my spoon. A euphoric rush pulsed through my veins, but it wasn't from a sugar high. I wanted to open up and tell all. And yet, I knew that whatever I was about to say would never capture the essence of my weekend. Something would get lost in the translation. I put my spoon in the empty cup and noticed Loretta was still waiting for me to speak.

"Did I tell you that Dan and Jason went on a camping trip last weekend?"

"I think you said something about that on the phone the last time we talked."

"I had three days all to myself. I can't remember the last time I've been home alone for more than a few hours. I felt as giddy as a kid at a carnival. So many fun options. I thought about getting a pedicure. Or meeting a friend for lunch. I even considered binge-watching season one of *Downton Abby*." I dipped the edge of a paper napkin into my water glass and wiped my sticky lips. "You know how we always talk about being with God and enjoying him?"

Loretta eyes widened as though she anticipated what I was about to say.

"I spent the weekend seeking God and fell in love with him all over again."

"That's wonderful, Honey! Tell me more."

"Honestly, when I woke up on Saturday I didn't know my weekend would turn into a three-day spiritual retreat. I went outside with my Bible and listened to praise music on my cell phone. But instead of reading my Bible and praying like I normally do, I started thanking God. I thanked him for my blessings. My family. My home. My friends. For good health and answered prayers. I thanked him for giving me the ability to communicate—for the chance to speak to women and for my last two articles that were published.

"Then something tugged my heart the same way my kids used to yank on my arm when they wanted to get my attention. I recognized the tug. It was the Holy Spirit. He gently said, 'Umm, Karen, did you notice that your gratitude is all about you? *Your* life, *your* gifts, *your* family—all the tangible things God has provided and done for *you*.' Being thankful is a good thing, but the Holy Spirit showed me that my praise revolved around me—when it should be all about God. So I asked the Spirit to examine my heart and point out any false motives. Was I praising God to earn his approval? Did I secretly hope for something in return—like more of his power so I could write better? Did I want some spiritual high?"

I glanced out the window and nodded towards the drive-through lane where people waited in their cars to place their orders. "I realized how often my prayers sound like I'm giving orders to God—as if he's a fast-food employee there to serve me. 'Get my article published. Give me a side of wisdom so I know how to speak to my kids, and double size my peace so I can get a good night's sleep. Make it quick. Please and thank you.'"

I cleared my throat. "Anyway, the 'tug' on my spirit humbled me. I got on my knees and apologized for being self-absorbed. I asked God to forgive me and to purify my motives. And you know what? I didn't picture him rolling his eyes at me in disgust. Instead, his overpowering love filled me and spilled out of me. I raised my hands and began praising God . . . and my praise didn't stem from penance or duty. I worshipped the Lord because he is worthy and deserves my praise. He's almighty God. I'm not."

I looked at Loretta and my next words came fast and hard, like water spewing from an uncapped fire hydrant. They flowed with force, as they had that day. "Praise just flowed from me non-stop. 'God, you are holy. You are the most high God who reigns forever. You are the God who sees. You are a God of compassion. You are merciful. You are just and true and more marvelous than my mind can comprehend.'"

I scooted closer to the wall to avoid the sun shining through the large-paned window. But it wasn't the sun that made my eyes water. Loretta reached into her purse, pulled out a tissue, and handed it to me.

"Loretta, I've had spiritual highs before but nothing like that day. When I focused on God, instead of myself, my view of him expanded. My praise was like a telephoto lens. When I zoomed in, I praised God for the life-giving breath that filled my lungs and his holy presence living in me. When I zoomed out, I praised God for his vastness—his supremacy and sovereignty over all the nations and the universe. The more I worshipped the Lord, the more humble and astounded I became that he would choose to love me and call me his own. He calls me his child. That is so endearing. He calls me the bride of Christ. That thought is mind-blowing! I spent the rest of the weekend totally immersed in God. I fasted.

I sang worship music. I listened for his voice as I read Scripture. By the time my guys returned home, my heart was full, satiated. I also felt victorious and fearless like I could take on the world."

I took a deep breath and laughed softly. "Sorry! I didn't mean to babble but hey, you asked."

Loretta smiled. "You can babble all you like. Your joy is contagious." Loretta inclined her head and studied my face. "Karen, do you realize how much you've changed since we first met?"

My neck grew warm and I tried to deflect the compliment heading my way. "Well, I do have a different hairdresser."

"Seriously, you're not the same woman that I met in Bible study a year ago. I see you praying and running to God first thing when you're overwhelmed. I see you making God more of a priority. I hear your joy when he's satisfied your heart." Loretta's voice turned husky. "You've become like a daughter to me. And if I love watching you become a woman after God's own heart, imagine how *he* feels when he sees you."

I looked up and blinked several times to hold back the tears. A pimple-faced teenager in a red polo shirt with an employee name tag walked by with a broom and black dustbin. I watched as she swept stiff French fries and crumbs into the dust bin's gaping mouth. Memories rushed back to me. I'd worked at McDonalds when I was about her age. It was around that time that I began to seek God in earnest. It'd been a long winding road since my teenage years but now I *knew* God in an intimate way that I could never have imagined back then.

"I have changed, Loretta. And I thank you for coming alongside me when God first nudged you to call me. When I think of everything we've talked about since we first began meeting, it really boils down to one thing—intimacy with God. I don't know if you remember, but you told me early on that you saw my hunger for God."

"I remember."

"You were spot on. I've always wanted to experience constant fellowship with the Lord throughout my day. My prayers were answered. I'm starting to sense his tangible presence more and more each day.

I rested my hands in my lap and sighed. "I know I can't always live on a spiritual high, but I sure don't want this oneness with God to end."

"Being one with God never ends, Karen. I believe," Loretta patted the spot just above her heart as if she were expressing the very beat of it, "that we become one with God the moment we believe in Jesus. The Holy Spirit comes and lives in us. He doesn't move. We are the ones who move. It's our choices that usually determine the depth of connection we feel with God."

Loretta looked at me, her animated brown eyes alive with light. "There's a certain rhythm to our oneness with God, don't you think? Sort of like a dance."

"A dance?" I questioned.

"Not literally, it's more of a metaphor." Loretta placed her two index fingers far apart on the table. "Until we fall in love with Jesus, we're far away. But then he calls us by name and we draw close to him." Loretta moved her two fingers next to each other. "God's Spirit is present, but we are independent creatures. We pull away and run after things we think will satisfy our hearts." Loretta moved one finger back a short distance. "Only, we don't move as far away from God as we once were. Then, whenever we're lonely or need God, we move towards him again and remain longer in his presence. Over time, the distance between us becomes shorter and *hopefully we learn* that only God satisfies our hearts." She entwined her two fingers as one and moved them rhythmically back and forth across the table. "And the more God satisfies our hearts, the more we want to stay near him . . . following his lead every day."

I watched her fingers glide back and forth like an elegant waltz, and my mind suddenly flitted to a powerful memory of Dan. I was in the kitchen making spaghetti sauce, when "Just the Way You Are" by Billy Joel came on the radio. Dan strolled into the kitchen and swept me into his arms. I'd protested, "My hands smell like garlic." But he pulled me close, gazed into my eyes, and sang the lyrics, "I love you just the way you are."

I melted into Dan's chest and breathed in his musky scent while we moved rhythmically to the music. When he waltzed me into the living room, we were like one body. I closed my eyes and listened to the music while we danced forwards and backwards around the room. I had no trouble following Dan because the tiniest pressure of his hand on my lower back or his left hand nudging mine signaled when he was about to change directions. In that moment, all thoughts of simmering spaghetti sauce vanished. I was caught up in a joyous place where nothing else existed but the two of us . . . and all because of a dance.

Was dancing with God any different? Sometimes I felt so close and in tune with God that I felt one with him. I'd feel a gentle press in my spirit telling me to go this way or that. Or I'd feel a nudge in my thoughts to call someone, write them a note, or take them a meal. Sometimes, he'd draw me close and tell me to rest, or wait. Jesus was leading me, it was my choice to follow or not.

But what if dancing with God had another dimension than remaining close to him and following his lead? What if I gave myself permission to literally dance before the Lord with all my might, like King David, when the Israelites brought the Ark of the Covenant back to Jerusalem? What if I responded like Miriam who shook her tambourine and danced to praise God when he brought the Israelites out of Egypt?

I nodded towards Loretta. "Have you ever danced before God? Literally or in your mind?"

She shook her head. "No, I'm too pragmatic. But sometimes I picture God sitting next to me on the couch. I also imagine myself sitting on the floor and kneeling against his leg. I'm totally at ease because God's a sweet, safe place where I can be myself. I can sing. I can cry and confess. I can be quiet. It's rosy cozy." Loretta patted her chest and her eyes filled with tears. "My heart is most satisfied when I'm with God and able to see myself the way he sees me—that I am loved!"

"You might be pragmatic, but I've noticed how you worship during church. You have a tissue in one hand to wipe your wet cheeks and your other hand is raised towards the ceiling."

She shrugged. "I love corporate worship. But I'm more reserved than many people. I was in my forties before I felt the freedom to raise my hands in church. Just my personality, I guess. Other people are more expressive in their worship. They kneel, shout, raise their hands, or dance. That's fine, but just because someone is more expressive about their worship doesn't make that person more spiritual than someone who may sit quietly in a chair. What matters to God is our heart's *genuine adoration*."

Loretta raked her long fingers through her wisps of feathery white hair. *So much wisdom and experience,* I thought. Gratitude welled in my chest for this safe, older woman who made the time to mentor me.

I glanced at my cell phone to check the time. "I wish we could keep talking, but I need to get home."

"Shoot bother, our visit was way too short."

"Short, but . . . definitely *sweet*." I said.

While Loretta excused herself to visit the restroom, I gathered our empty ice cream cups and threw them in the trash.

Later, outside, we stood beside Loretta's car and shaded our eyes from the sun's brightness.

"Karen, I loved hearing about your weekend. Thanks for sharing. It blessed my heart."

I pulled Loretta into a hug. "I'm over the moon that you're my sister in Christ because we'll be together in heaven. And you know what that means?" I stepped back, held her firmly by the shoulders, and looked intently into her curious eyes. "You're *never* getting rid of me."

Loretta threw back her head and laughed hard. If she hadn't been so pragmatic, I would have grabbed her hands and twirled her in the parking lot. Instead, I pulled a small, white paper bag from my oversized purse and gave it to her.

"I bought you a gift."

Loretta's eyes widened when she looked inside. "You spoil me."

"Eat 'em while they're hot." I said and hurried away before I was tempted to go back inside and buy some French fries for myself.

In the days that followed I thought much about what it meant to "dance with God." One morning I was home alone, unloading the dishwasher. Praise music played in the background. The song, "I Can Only Imagine" by Mercy Me, began to play. I set down the spatula in my hand and sang along. "Surrounded by your glory, what will my heart feel? Will I dance for you, Jesus? Or, in awe of you be still?"

As I swayed to the melody my heart seemed to soar to another place in time. I was in my kitchen, but not. My bare feet glided across the cool wooden floor but, when I looked down, I envisioned standing on a translucent lake. Flecks of light glistened like diamonds on the ripply water. And Jesus stood next to me, his nail-pierced hands extended in invitation.

"Karen, you are my beloved bride," He whispered. **"Shall we dance?"**

I looked into his love-filled eyes. Reflected in them I saw myself. I was surprised by how I appeared. I was radiant, glowing. I wore a flowing calf-length white dress covered in satin lace and pearl beads. A laurel of wildflowers encircled my head like a crown.

"I'd love to dance."

Jesus took my hand and I instinctively knew how to move with him. We twirled and leapt upon the water as though we were two figure ice skaters moving in sync. Giant redwoods surrounded the lake like tall sentries. I inhaled their fresh pine scent. When we danced closer to the shore, I saw a white gazebo with twinkling gold lights braided in between the lattice work. Inside the gazebo was a round table covered with a royal blue linen cloth, and in the center of the table stood a vase filled with cheerful sunflowers.

Tears mingled with laughter. I sensed an indescribable oneness with Jesus. As I looked into his eyes, joy bubbled inside of me until my heart felt like a bottle of champagne whose cork was about to explode.

"Sweet Jesus, I adore you. Your faithfulness and love for me is more precious than anything I could ever want or hope for. I am blessed beyond words. Whenever I think about our relationship and how I'm one with your Spirit, I'm in awe that you'd choose me to be your beloved bride. Jesus, you are my King and the Lord of my life! There is no one like—"

Ow!

My shin collided with the open dishwasher door and swept me back to reality. I limped to my kitchen stool and crawled up on it. But the sting of pain couldn't dim the ecstatic joy inside me. For I knew that Jesus loved me even when I danced like I had two left feet.

As I rubbed my scraped shin I prayed out loud, "Thank You, Lord, for turning my messy kitchen into a sacred place. Help me to dance before you, and with you, like a bride enchanted by her one true love. We both know I will stumble and fall. I may step on your toes. But by your grace, as long as I have breath, may I continue to dance in your presence. One step and one glorious song at a time."

Take Away Nuggets

 Nothing satisfies your soul like dancing with Jesus.

 "Praise his name with dancing; accompanied by tambourine and harp" (Psalm 149:3).

Food for Thought

1. Karen took time to examine her true motives about why she was praising God. What changed for her when she shifted her prayer focus away from herself and to God? When you are alone with God, what percent of your time is focused on your own needs and desires? What percent is spent focusing solely on God?

2. Dancing with God looked differently for Karen than it did for Loretta. Are you more expressive in action, like Karen, who actually swirled around her kitchen like a bride in love? Or is your dance of oneness more in your mind, like Loretta, who was outwardly less expressive but inwardly alive to God? Write a paragraph to describe what your own dance with God looks like?

3. What is the difference between dancing with a stranger and dancing with someone you care deeply about? How does this idea motivate you to want to know God in a deeper way?

4. Are there any barriers that would keep you from dancing? Read Psalm 30:11 and Psalm 149:3. Can you describe a time like this that happened to you?

CHAPTER 11

Satisfied Heart

"For he satisfies the longing soul, and the hungry soul he fills with good things" (Psalm 107:9 ESV).

December 2018, Sutter General Hospital

I lay in a hospital bed hooked to an IV. The bag of fluid hanging from the stand beside me drips fear down a plastic tube and into my veins through a needle lodged in my wrist.

I try to pray the fear away, *Jesus, help me! I'm so weak. I need to feel your strong presence!* But the fear keeps dripping in.

I shiver and pull my chilly hands beneath the blue flimsy blanket. My thin hospital gown and socks aren't warm enough. I need another blanket. One other patient occupies this sterile, dimly lit room. We each lie in our own private pain, separated by a sage-green curtain too thin to muffle the elderly woman's tiny moans. I turn my head towards the picture window. The shade is down but, no matter, the sun set hours ago. I yawn, then take a deep breath. My pillowcase smells like antiseptic. I reposition my head and watch the second hand on the wall clock march in endless circles while I count my blessings.

Thank God, I'm alive! But, this isn't what I'd imagined doing during the Christmas season. I close my eyes, wishing for what might have been—Dan and I rendezvousing with our two sons in Georgia where Jenny and her husband live. I long to touch Jen's belly ripe with the life of our first grandchild.

I swallow hard. Will I be well enough to travel and see my grandson's face?

The *squeak, squeak, squeak* of rubber-soled shoes moves across the linoleum floor as someone enters the room. A flurry of clicking sounds like fingernails hitting laptop keys. *Can you help me?* Before I can form the words to ask for another blanket, the squeaker is gone. Tears prick my eyes. I shift stiff arms and legs to find a more comfortable position on the hard mattress, but the cardiac leads and wires attached to my chest make it difficult.

I can't believe I just got a stent in my heart's main artery. But that stent will supposedly save my life. The memory of my heart banging wildly against my chest a few weeks ago is still fresh. I shudder. What if my heart attack had killed me that day?

But it didn't.

What if I have another heart attack?

I know the answer.

My days are in God's hands. The thought vanquishes the fear that's been dripping into my veins and a surreal peace begins to flow through me. I look at the clock whose hands align to twelve (midnight) and wonder, *What if this had been my last day?* Seeing Jesus face to face in time for Christmas? What an incredible gift! Oh, to be with the One I've spent my life pursuing! I long to hear him say, "Well done, Karen, my good and faithful servant. Enter into my rest."

My pulse quickens. Am I ready to leave this earth? What about my bucket list? Have I finished the tasks God asked me to do? Am I ready to kiss my family goodbye and entrust them to the Lord? I dig my fingernails into the bed's starched sheet as if that could somehow tether me to this world. I'm not afraid of death as much as leaving my loved ones behind. I don't want to miss being part of their lives. I feel some pressing need to be here for them.

Then, comes a moment of reckoning. Have I made the most of my life? Have I loved well? Made a difference? Hundreds of faces, images, moments in time, flash through my mind in a heartbeat. Sixty-three years of my life pressed into a thumbnail composite.

I weep happy tears. My heavenly Father who's been faithful to me will take care of my family. My fingers uncurl. I've had a wonderful life! There's little I'd change. I'm so blessed. Accepting Loretta's invitation to mentor me was one of my biggest blessings. Loretta's wisdom helped me live better in this life and prepared me for whatever is next. I hear her challenge in my head, "Ask God to teach you *no matter the cost.*"

What is the cost? A stent? Missing Christmas with my family?

Yes, I can say that now . . . without crossing my fingers.

What if the cost is my life?

I remember the cost Jesus paid at Calvary to save me. I remember God's deep, unwavering love for me. My body relaxes.

"Lord, my heart belongs to you! Whether you choose to have me stay here, or whether you choose to call me home to be with you, I'm ready because I trust you even in this."

When I had a heart attack, I didn't know if I'd ever type the final words of this book. But God decided to give me a little more time here on planet earth. As I reflect on the lessons Loretta taught me, I'm forever grateful. Loretta mentored me, but the Holy Spirit pursued me and did my heart work. To God be the glory. Here are my lessons in a nutshell:

- ☐ Ask God to teach and change me no matter the cost.
- ☐ To the degree that I want God is the degree that I'll seek him.
- ☐ God welcomes my questions, but he doesn't have to justify his actions.
- ☐ Giant faith is built through baby steps of trust.
- ☐ God's love for me is eternal and unwavering.
- ☐ My identity is not based on the opinion of others, but on God's radical love for me.
- ☐ The purpose of life is to become like Jesus.
- ☐ When I can't see God's face, I need to trust his heart.
- ☐ Pray for people's character growth instead of only specifics.
- ☐ Nothing satisfies my soul like dancing with Jesus.

Loretta and I still get together for lunch. God continues to meet us right where we are—the learning never ends. During one of our meals, somewhere between the appetizer and dessert, Loretta looked at me with her smiling eyes and said, "Karen, I've taught you everything I know. Time for you to pass on what you've learned to others."

Consider it done, my friend. Consider it done.

Dinner Mints

Early on whenever I met with Loretta, I'd leave our lunches feeling spiritually satisfied but mentally stuffed. Our rich God-filled conversations were a lot for me to digest in a two-hour conversation.

Perhaps you feel the same way after reading *Lunch with Loretta*. So many lessons, too much to absorb. I'd be remiss if I didn't offer you dinner mints (often served after a meal to soothe the stomach, help with digestion, and leave a sweet taste in your mouth). Only instead of round red and white mints, I want to offer you the sweetest, most soothing truth I can share—the truth that God loves you, and he sent his Son, Jesus, to die for you so you could live in fellowship with him all the days of your life. These verses explain God's amazing plan to make that happen.

"For everyone has sinned; we all fall short of God's glorious standards" (Romans 3:23).

"For the wages of sin is death, but the free gift of God is eternal life through Christ Jesus our Lord" (Romans 6:23).

"And this is what God has testified: he has given us eternal life, and this life is in his Son. Whoever has the Son has life, whoever does not have God's Son does not have life" (1 John 5:11-12).

"If you openly declare that Jesus is Lord and believe in your heart that God raised him from the dead, you will be saved. For it is by believing in your heart that you are made right with God, and it is by openly declaring your faith that you are saved" (Romans 10: 9-11).

"Each of you must repent of your sins and turn to God, and be baptized in the name of Jesus Christ for the forgiveness of your sins. Then you will receive the gift of the Holy Spirit" (Acts 2:38).

Do you want to be right with God? Do you want to be forgiven? Do you want to have eternal life? Do you want the power of God's Holy Spirit living in you? If so, you can start right now by praying a simple prayer.

Prayer: God, I confess I'm a sinner. I need your forgiveness. I believe Jesus died on the cross to pay for my sins, and that he rose from the dead so that I may have eternal life. Jesus, I invite you to come into my heart. I want to trust and follow you as Lord of my life. Amen.

Dear friend, if you prayed that prayer, I'm excited for you. Doing life with Jesus has been the greatest thrill of my life. I pray that, like me, you'll discover the wonderful truth that Jesus can indeed satisfy the hunger in your soul.

With love,
Karen

You can reach and follow me at:
karenfosterauthor.com
karenyfoster@gmail.com

Recipes

Food is a great communicator, connecting generations and helping build memories and friendships. It gathers us together and teaches us the importance of sharing not just food, but ourselves.
—Rachael Ray

Loretta's Carrot Cake

An old, old recipe from a friend, BEST EVER!

Ingredients for Cake:

- ☐ 2 cups flour
- ☐ 2 cups sugar
- ☐ 2 tsp. baking soda
- ☐ 2 tsp. cinnamon
- ☐ 2 tsp. nutmeg
- ☐ 1/4 tsp. ginger
- ☐ 1/2 tsp. cloves
- ☐ 1 1/2 cups oil
- ☐ 4 beaten eggs
- ☐ 1 tsp. vanilla
- ☐ 3 cups shredded carrots
- ☐ 1 20 oz can of crushed pineapple (drained)
- ☐ 1 cup chopped walnuts

Directions:

Preheat oven to 350 degrees, and coat a 9x13 baking pan with cooking spray.

Mix the first ten cake ingredients. Add the carrots, pineapple, and walnuts last. Pour batter in pan. Bake 45 minutes (Check w toothpick or lightly touch cake. Should spring back.)

Blend ingredients for Frosting

- ☐ 1 cube butter
- ☐ 1 box powdered sugar
- ☐ 8 oz pkg. cream cheese

Exodus 33:13 has been my life verse. "If I have found favor in your sight, show me your ways that I may know you." That became my focus and goal. Coupled with that, there is nothing sweeter in life than passing onto another what the Creator of the universe has taught me about Himself. With Karen, He alone sent me to the Bible study she attended. He alone let me see her desire for Him. He alone spoke to me and asked that I "come alongside." He alone never missed a time when we met. He alone spoke through this empty vessel on every occasion. He alone proved His presence and accomplished His purposes in each of us. Happily, as I look back, I see the same repeated over and over in the lives of so many He brought into my life. My LABC kids and many others with their unique stories. He the initiator and enabler brought a sweet mutuality that benefited each of us. God has always been at the center of it all.

Loretta Chalfant

Linda's Blueberry Cobbler

Gluten Free, easy, bursting with flavor

Ingredients:

- ☐ 4 cups blueberries (fresh or frozen)
- ☐ Cobbler Topping: (Mix together in a bowl)
- ☐ 1 cup gluten free or regular rolled oats
- ☐ ½ cup chopped pecans
- ☐ ½ cup almond flour (or other flour)
- ☐ ¼ cup maple syrup
- ☐ ¼ cup olive oil
- ☐ ½ tsp. salt.

Directions

Layer blueberries and cobbler topping in an 8x8 pan. Bake 40 minutes at 350 degrees.

God has given me the privilege to mentor many women through my writing and teaching on marriage and sexuality. God called me to walk many of his most wounded women through their journey to healing from sexual abuse. My method of mentoring is not based on a program. Instead, I get on my knees with women and take them before the throne of God as we worship and read the Scripture together.

Linda Dillow, missionary, speaker, and author of multiple books including *Calm My Anxious Heart* and *Intimate Issues.*

Barb's Bed and Breakfast
Corn Flake Potatoes

Who needs milk when you can have cereal on hash browns

Ingredients:

- ☐ 1 cup of butter
- ☐ 1 medium onion (chopped)
- ☐ 1 package frozen hash browns (32 oz)
- ☐ 1 can mushroom soup (10 3/4 oz)
- ☐ 1 pint sour cream
- ☐ 2 cups of shredded mild cheddar cheese
- ☐ 3 cups of cornflakes

Directions:

Preheat oven to 350 degrees

Sauté 1/2 cup butter, chopped onion, and hash brown potatoes in large pan.

In a separate bowl, mix the mushroom soup, sour cream, and shredded mild cheddar cheese. Add sautéed items to the soup mixture and stir well. Pour mixture into a 9 x13 baking dish. Bake for 50 minutes.

A few minutes prior to potatoes being done, sauté 3 cups of cornflakes in 1/2 cup of butter.

Remove baking dish from oven and spread sautéed cornflakes on top of casserole. Bake an additional 3-4 minutes. Serves 12.

Loretta and I were neighbors when she walked into my crisis-filled life over forty years ago. Through her gentle and loving wise counsel, Loretta showed me a holy, sovereign God who loved me. But it was Loretta's consistent, never doubting faith that caused me to earnestly seek God and know him more fully. Loretta didn't just teach me how to listen to God's voice and obey him, her actions showed me what obedience looks like. I've watched Loretta choose joy in the worst of times because she knows the "Joy Giver" and "He is enough." Some may call that mentoring, but for me, Loretta is an answer to a prayer.

Barbara Franchino, owns Elam Biggs Bed & Breakfast. elambiggs.com

Liz's Favorite Glazed Lemon Bread

An easy recipe for a moist and lemony treat

Ingredients:

- ☐ 3 cups all-purpose flour
- ☐ 2 cups sugar
- ☐ 2 tsp. baking powder
- ☐ 1 tsp. salt
- ☐ 4 large eggs
- ☐ 1 cup milk
- ☐ 1 cup salad oil
- ☐ 3 tsp. grated lemon peel

Directions:

In a large bowl, stir together flour, sugar, baking powder, and salt. In a small bowl, lightly beat eggs, then beat in milk, oil, and lemon peel. Add liquid mixture to flour mixture and stir just until blended. Pour batter into two greased, flour-dusted 5x9 inch loaf pans. Bake in a 350 degree oven until a wooden pick inserted in center comes out clean (40-45 minutes).

When bread is done, use a long wooden skewer to poke numerous holes all the way to the bottom of loaves. Drizzle hot Lemon Glaze over top so that it slowly soaks into bread. Let bread cool in pan on a rack for about 15 minutes, then turn out onto rack and let cool completely. Makes 2 loaves.

Lemon Glaze: In a small pan, combine 1/2 cup plus 1 tablespoon lemon juice and 2/3 cups sugar. Stir over medium heat until sugar is dissolved.

I met Loretta Chalfant in the early 1970s when she was the bookstore manager at the college I attended. I spent many hours confiding in her, asking questions, and soaking up her wisdom about life, love, and the Father. A decade later, I sought Loretta's guidance about a possible career change. Knowing my love of books, she suggested I apply for an editing job. I did and was offered a job as an entry level editor. Turns out editing was the perfect job for me. I'm still at it, all these many years later. Thank you, Loretta ... for your love and confidence in me and for always pointing me to the sovereignty of God.

Liz Heaney

Mary's Arugula, Beet and Goat Cheese Salad

Easy-prep salad is a delicious meatless entree

Ingredients:

- ☐ 1 bag of pre-washed arugula
- ☐ 3 to 4 beets (red or golden)
- ☐ 3 oz. goat cheese
- ☐ capers (optional)

Dressing ingredients:

- ☐ 1/4 cup balsamic vinegar
- ☐ 1/2 cup good olive oil
- ☐ 2 tsp. Dijon mustard
- ☐ salt & pepper to taste

Directions:

Preheat oven to 400 degrees.

Cut tops off beets. Scrub the beets and peel any rough parts but otherwise leave as much skin as possible. Place parchment paper on a cutting board (to prevent stains) and cut the beets into same-size chunks.

Drizzle beets with olive oil, salt and pepper. Mix with your hands. Place beets on a sheet pan and roast for 20-30 minutes or until tender.

Meanwhile, whisk together the vinegar, olive oil, mustard, salt and pepper. Set aside. I often make it in a jar and shake it. Sometimes I add a tad of honey.

In a salad bowl, put arugula and roasted beets (warm or room temperature). Add crumbled goat cheese and toss with the dressing. Sprinkle with capers.

I'm part of Loretta's legacy because she mentored Karen who mentored me. Spiritual mentoring has been my life-saver: offering a stream of deep truth, age-old wisdom, and accountability that nourished me during struggles that could have otherwise derailed me. This trickle down effect from one mentor to another had a lasting impact. It caused me to fall in love with the Lord and experience his joy.

Mary Stivender, amateur naturalist and Marketing Associate Director

Phyllis's Salmon Potato Delight

An easy gourmet go-to favorite

Ingredients:

- ☐ 2 sweet potatoes, peeled and cubed
- ☐ 1 lb. small red potatoes quartered
- ☐ ¼ cup olive oil
- ☐ Salt, pepper
- ☐ ½ cup prepared pesto sauce
- ☐ 1 lb. salmon, whole or in four 4-ounce portions (frozen or fresh)

Directions:

Combine cut red and sweet potatoes in a bowl. Add olive oil, salt, and pepper. Stir until all potatoes are coated. Roast in oven at 375 degrees for 30 minutes.

Spread roasted potatoes in 8x10 baking dish. Lay salmon on top of potatoes. Spread pesto sauce liberally over salmon. Bake at 350 for about 25 minutes. Serve with a salad or vegetable. *Voila!* An impressive tasty meal that is easy and nutritious!

My husband encouraged me to reproduce in others what I'd learned about Jesus. As a result, I've spent the last fifty years discipling and mentoring other women. I think of discipleship as meeting with a small group of women, or one on one, to share the basic principles of the Christian life so they can grow and pass it on. Mentoring is spending time individually with a woman who wants to grow in a particular area. Each year I asked God for "one" woman. Often I tailored the material we covered for her needs. After my four children were grown, I asked God to give me small groups—six to ten women. Usually I took them through material like *Lessons on Assurance* (5 week program by NavPress) or *Five Aspects of Woman* by Barbara Mouser. One of my life's greatest joys has been to mentor three of my granddaughters. We must seek not only to live the message of the gospel, but to pass our hope on to others.

Phyllis Stanley

Beckie's Pasta Salad

Packed with veggies and an Italian twang

Ingredients:

- ☐ 1 lb. curly (corkscrew) pasta
- ☐ 5 Roma tomatoes diced
- ☐ 1 6 oz. can sliced black olives
- ☐ 1 handful green olives sliced
- ☐ 1 small onion chopped (any kind)
- ☐ 1 cucumber chopped
- ☐ 1 green pepper chopped
- ☐ 1 jar of salad supreme seasoning (I use half)
- ☐ 1 15 oz. bottle Italian dressing

Directions:

Cook the pasta and drain well.

Meanwhile, cut up veggies and place in a large bowl. Pour the dressing and seasoning over the veggies and stir well. Add cooked pasta to the bowl and stir.

Place in fridge and stir occasionally throughout the day.

Pasta salad will stay fresh in fridge for a week.

I asked Loretta to mentor me when I was newly married because I wanted to know God more intimately and have a better prayer life. Loretta agreed to meet with me once a week for several years. Using Scripture, she showed me how me to pursue Christ and to encourage the people in my life. She also prayed with me and shared worship songs whenever I felt anxious. Loretta's Biblical wisdom and her insight on Christian principles were inspirational and helped me grow spiritually. Asking Loretta to be my mentor was a wise decision.

Beckie Ruggles

Liz's Chopped Salad

An anything goes, personalized salad

Ingredients:

- Romaine lettuce
- Butter lettuce
- mixed greens
- hard boiled eggs, sliced
- cherry tomatoes
- pecans or walnuts, chopped
- garbanzo or kidney beans (drained)
- salami, thinly sliced

- purple onion, thinly slice
- cucumbers, sliced
- fresh mozzarella balls (small)
- baby carrots
- blue cheese crumbles
- avocado
- bell peppers (variety of colors) chopped
- black olives, chopped

Directions:

Put the salad greens and the individual toppings in separate bowls. Each person selects her favorite ingredients and puts them into a large bowl. Toss with dressing. Put the salad mixture onto a cutting board and chop into smaller pieces. Transfer to the individual's plate.

Homemade Ranch Dressing:

Combine all the ingredients and stir.

- 1/2 cup mayonnaise
- 1/2 cup buttermilk
- 1/2 tsp Worcestershire sauce
- 1/2 tsp. dried parsley
- 1/2 tsp. onion powder
- 1/2 tsp. garlic powder
- 1 clove garlic crushed

- 1/2 tsp. dried dill weed (optional)
- 1/4 tsp. salt
- 1/8 tsp. pepper
- Add extra buttermilk or milk if the dressing is too thick.

A joy of mine is encouraging women with Christ's love and the truths of God's Word. Mentoring was modeled to me over twenty years by a precious woman named Ruth Hill. She's with the Lord now, but I watched Ruth pour herself into the lives of so many women over the years including mine. She was incredibly faithful, authentic, available, and teachable. Ruth's mentoring style was life on life. We spent countless hours sharing meals, shopping together, talking on the phone. She welcomed me into her home and her heart. As life unfolded, we talked about life, the books we read, our struggles. Ruth would weave Scripture and what the Lord had been teaching her into our conversation while pointing me to my heavenly Father. I miss her!

Liz Ziegenmeyer, Registered Nurse

Lori's Spinach/Chard/Kale Souffle

Crustless, low-carb yumminess

Ingredients:

- ☐ 3 eggs
- ☐ 3 Tb. flour
- ☐ 12 oz. cottage cheese
- ☐ 2/3 lb. any shredded cheese (especially good with fresh Asiago & Parmesan)
- ☐ 2 tsp. garlic
- ☐ 1 tsp. of Italian seasoning
- ☐ 6 Tb.butter (melted)
- ☐ 4 oz. fresh spinach, chard, kale

Directions:

Mix all ingredients and place in a greased 2 qt casserole dish

Bake at 350 for about 45 minutes

Double this in a 9x13 pan

Delicious add-ins: cooked bacon, sausage, ham, any other pre-cooked veggies.

Mrs. C was the listening ear and the words of wisdom to anyone who walked in the LABC bookstore. One year I asked if she would "mentor" me. She paused and said, "Well, I did pray that God would give me a little more." I responded, "I'll be your Little Moore." (Moore is my maiden name.) We didn't use a specific program or study. We met now and then to chat about life, love, decisions, and following God. I cannot think of Mrs. C without remembering all of the wisdom and love that goes with her. Outside of my family, she has been the most influential person in my life.

Lori Payton, pastor's wife

Sue's Chicken Caesar Wraps

Compliments of her sister, Lori Payton
– also mentored by Loretta

Ingredients for chicken marinade:

- ☐ 1 1b. boneless, skinless chicken breasts
- ☐ 3 Tb. olive oil
- ☐ 1 tsp. lemon pepper
- ☐ 1 tsp. crushed garlic
- ☐ 1/2 tsp. of Italian seasoning

Ingredients for Caesar dressing:

- ☐ 1 cup sour cream (lite)
- ☐ 2 Tb. milk
- ☐ 3 Tb. grated Parmesan cheese
- ☐ 1/2 tsp. of Italian seasoning
- ☐ 1/2 tsp. pepper
- ☐ 1/2 tsp. crushed garlic

Directions:

Combine the first four ingredients in a large plastic storage bag. Add chicken, seal, and shake to mix. Refrigerate at least 15 minutes.

Preheat gas grill to medium heat. (George Foreman also works.) Grill or broil in oven 10-20 minutes, turning occasionally. Remove and cut into strips.

Mix ingredients for Caesar dressing in small bowl.

Place chopped Romaine lettuce and sliced chicken in a warmed flour tortilla. Top with dressing and fold tortilla. Makes 4 servings.

Add a fruit salad, chips, or rice pilaf for heartier eaters.

 Loretta Chalfant worked at our college bookstore and was lovingly known as the "bookstore lady." She always offered students wisdom, love and laughter. We needed all three. Loretta mentored me while I attended college. I saw how it made all the difference in my walk with Jesus to be encouraged by an older, wiser woman. Consequently, I began mentoring high school girls in my twenties. For me, the key to mentorship is humility, sitting at Jesus' feet and listening to him. That way, whatever is poured into a younger believer is something worthwhile. I was blessed to have Loretta pour herself into me. I'm honored to call her friend and mentor.

Sue Donaldson, welcomeheart.com

Susan's Chicken Tomato Dish

Excellent and effortless entree

Ingredients:

- ☐ 6-8 boneless chicken thighs/legs (or 4 boneless chicken breasts)
- ☐ 1 15 oz. can tomatoes (stewed, diced, or seasoned) partially drained
- ☐ 1 Tb. vegetable or canola oil (optional)
- ☐ 1-2 Tb. ground sage (to taste)
- ☐ 2 tsp. oregano
- ☐ 1 tsp. celery salt
- ☐ 2 Tb. minced onion or 1/2 chopped yellow onion
- ☐ 1 cup chicken broth

Directions:

Preheat oven to 350 degrees.

Put chicken in a 10 x 13 pan. Mix other ingredients in small bowl. Pour seasoned mixture over the meat.

Cover with aluminum foil and bake for 30 minutes. Remove foil and bake 15 minutes longer. Baste every fifteen minutes.

If chicken is frozen, bake 40 minutes before removing foil and then another 20 minutes. Bone in will add more baking time by at least 10-15 minutes.

Serve over rice.

I have been mentored by three wonderful women over more than 35 years and had the opportunity to mentor over 25 women. Mentoring is a lifestyle which involves keeping eyes open to opportunities, ears listening for conversation, and a heart desiring to share God's love and all he has taught me. Mentoring is one of the greatest blessings in my life. These one-on-one relationships allow me to encourage women in their relationship with God and pray for them as we share life together.

Susan Sage, writer of devotionals and flash fiction at susansage.com.

Mindy's Curry Chicken Salad

A simple, healthy dish her husband Vic also enjoys making

Ingredients for Salad:

- ☐ 2 boneless chicken breasts cooked and chopped (fried, grilled, or baked)
- ☐ 1/2 cup dried cranberries
- ☐ 1/3 cup chopped roasted pecans
- ☐ 1/3 cup diced celery

Ingredients for Dressing:

- ☐ 1/3 cup mayonnaise
- ☐ 1/3 cup sour cream
- ☐ 1 Tb. lemon juice
- ☐ 1/2 tsp. curry powder
- ☐ salt and pepper to taste

Directions:

Combine chopped chicken breasts, cranberries, pecans, and celery in a bowl. Mix dressing ingredients and pour over chicken salad. Serve on top of apple slices or thin apple rounds.

Mentoring is a fantastic way to build one another up in Christ, to give back what God has taught us, and learn how to navigate life from someone who has been there. Mentoring is the opposite of what Satan wants. He prefers to keep Christians alone in our spiritual walk so we'll stay weak instead of allowing us to come together. You don't have to live in the same state to have a mentor or be one. For the past ten years, Loretta and Karen have both mentored me via phone calls and email. They're a blessing from God.

Mindy Nichols, homeschool mom

Judi's Chilled Broccoli Salad

Quick summer salad to make ahead of time

Ingredients:

- ☐ 2 bunches of fresh broccoli (trimmed and cut into pieces)
- ☐ 1 cup fresh parsley, chopped
- ☐ 2 or 3 green onions, sliced
- ☐ 1/2 cup of skim or nonfat cottage cheese
- ☐ 1/4 cup of light mayonnaise
- ☐ 1/2 cup of skim milk
- ☐ 1 clove garlic, minced
- ☐ 3/4 tsp. dill weed

Directions:

Blanch broccoli for five minutes in boiling water. Toss with parsley and onions.

Make dressing by blending cottage cheese, mayonnaise, milk, garlic, and dill until smooth.

Toss with vegetables and chill well.

Optional: dried cranberries or sunflower seeds

Makes eight servings.

Being mentored is a special gift to us from our loving Father. The following words spoken into my life had a profound impact on who I became in Christ. "Nothing you do, or not do, will ever increase or decrease the magnitude of the love Jesus has shown for you on the cross."

Judi Minke

Kathleen's Powdered Sugar Donuts

No Cook, No Cleanup, No Excuse

Ingredients:

- ☐ Donuts from your favorite bakery (variety is best, but powdered sugar is a winner)
- ☐ Coffee or tea from your favorite brewer
- ☐ Napkins

Directions:

Pick up donuts and coffee. Meet friend at a pre-arranged casual and comfortable location.

Servings: Let your conscience be your guide.

Optional: Pastry (in Los Angeles, Porto's the place)

Loretta mentored me while I attended LABC along with other students clamoring for her words of wisdom. I'd buy a package of powdered sugar donuts in the college bookstore where Loretta worked and share them with her over some "lofty" conversation about Winnie the Pooh or Oswald Chambers—equally wise, I might add. Since then, my passion (which I credit Loretta for encouraging in me) is to share "firm faith" with Christian women who live in fear or lack confidence. And encouraging women to speak God's truth to their hearts when fears arise. This is the way I have discipled my four grown daughters over the years. And to be honest, my mentoring style is "love the one you're with." In other words, I love pouring into whoever God brings across my path today. For me, mentoring means being available even at a moment's notice: "Sure! I can meet you today for coffee and a chat." And then allowing God's Spirit to take it from there!

Kathleen Thomson, teacher for women's Bible studies.

Acknowledgements

I have to laugh. I balked when Loretta challenged me to ask God to teach and change me no matter the cost. So God, knowing I'm a fearful creature, used my writing as a means to teach and change me. Thankfully the Lord sent plenty of folks along my path to equip and challenge me to finish this book.

Loretta Chalfant: Thank you for not only mentoring me, but allowing me to put your words and life on public display. I picked, pushed, prodded you to remember details you might have preferred to forget. It scrambles my eggs when I consider how often you've prayed for me and this book.

Lorraine Pintus: Thank you for making a dream come true. I may have given birth to this book, but your expertise as a writing coach enabled me to raise this baby to maturity. You recognized the eternal value of this book's message, and you made sure I owned the truths I wrote about. Keep dancing!

Terri Jorgenson: Years ago, you introduced me to Lorraine. Then you urged me to attend my first writer's conference with you when this book was in its embryonic stage. Thank you for those timely prayers over the phone. I'd like to give you all the credit for resurfacing whenever I needed you, but we both know those seemingly random moments were a God thing.

Diane Danielson: You encouraged me from day one to pursue my dream. The kick in my pants came when you challenged me, "Why not hire a writing coach?" Do you realize how you motivated me all these years by simply asking me questions and brainstorming?

To my Inspire Christian Writer's critique group: Bonnie Arbaugh, Carole Barber, Sarah Barnum, Jacqui Bennett, Abby Drinen, Rosemary Johnson, Kris Lindsey, Bethany Macklin, Robynne Miller, Karen Pickrell, Dina Preuss, Susan Sage, Karen Schubert, Deborah Silva, and Libby Worden. Thanks for reading multiple drafts of this book and providing input. Your pep talks kept me from deleting my files.

To my Beta readers who provided me an extra set of eyes prior to publication: Sarah Barnum, Abby Drinen, Bailey Gillespie, Betty Hightower, Terri Jorgenson, Jan Kern, Kris Lindsey, Bethany Macklin, Barb Raveling, and Susan Sage. Thank you for donating your valuable time and insight. I owe you.

To my forever friends and faithful prayer warriors: Rather than include some and risk omitting others, I count on you to know who you are. Thank you for cheering me towards the finish line. Your friendship and support is a wonderful gift.

To the women who contributed recipes: Whether you were the mentor or mentee, I appreciate your insights about the value of a mentoring relationship. I've tested your recipes and gained the pounds to prove it. Kudos!

Walt and Yvonne: I couldn't ask for more wonderful, supportive parents. Thanks to you, I fell in love with books and learned to appreciate people's stories. You welcomed Jesus into our home and showed me first hand how to love well. By the way, Randy says you love him more. We'll let him keep thinking that. Maybe one day he'll write a song about his favorite sibling.

Matthias: I know you won't read this book. That's why they have audio books.

Jonathan, Jennifer, and Jason: I love you to the moon and back. And I love, love, love being your mom. If it weren't for you in my life, I'd be on my third book. Then again, without your technical savvy and "Attagirl Mom," I'd still be using a typewriter.

Captain Dan: After forty-one years of marriage, we have the perfect arrangement. You don't make me fly with you and I don't make you read what I write. Thank you for giving me the freedom and uninterrupted space to write this book. How sweet it is to be your Goodbye Girl!

Axel: You're just now learning to walk, and I pray that one day you'll meet Jesus and want to walk with him. Just remember, Jesus is so much more than a one-dimensional piece of felt on a flannel gram. And there's only one book you *need* to read—God's Word.

Jesus: I love you. Thank you for loving me first and making yourself known—even in this.

About the Author

Maybe it's the bookworm or thespian in me, but I see life as a giant storyboard. I've never known a time when I wasn't reading and writing stories. Or, performing in someone's story on stage which is why I have a college degree in Speech and Theater Arts. I also love studying God's Word. So yeah, *words* play a huge role in my life.

I grew up as a military brat so joining the Air Force after college as a Public Affairs Officer seemed fitting. I married a pilot, who's kept my heart soaring for 41 years, and exchanged my combat boots for baby booties as our family of two grew to five. In fact, my freelance writing career began when I caught the chicken pox from my toddlers and wrote a devotional for *The Upper Room* about the experience.

Since then, I've written devotions, articles, and feature stories for newspapers and magazines. I particularly love ghostwriting people's true-life stories and giving them a voice. I've also been a contributor to *Chicken Soup for the Soul: Military Families* (May 2017), *The Horse of Our Dreams: True Stories of the Horses We Love* (Revell 2019), and seven Inspire Christian Writers' anthologies.

Being a wife and mom is my greatest joy. Other roles that define me: Event's speaker, homeschool mom (six years), Bible study leader,

Drama teacher, Jail chaplain, volunteer for pro-life and homeless ministries, board member of Inspire Christian Writers.

Now, I'm in a new chapter. My children are grown, my husband is retired, and I'm having a blast being a grandma. But, the Word remains my first Love. Check out my website and blog: karenfosterauthor.com.